MW01225307

No Other Option: Self-Determination for Alberta

By Michael Wagner

REVIEWS

Michael Wagner is one of the authoritative voices on the Alberta and Western independence movements. His previous book, *Alberta Separatism: Then and Now* is the go-to resource for anyone looking for a concise history of the topic. For almost a year, he has been a regular senior contributor to the Western Standard where he has published insightful histories, explanations, and observations of the independence movement. In *No Other Option*, Wagner combines his considerable knowledge of the independence movement's history with a strong case for why it is the correct path forward for Alberta, and potentially the broader West.

Derek Fildebrandt is the Publisher of the *Western Standard*

A little over a year ago I read Michael Wagner's book *Alberta: Separatism Then and Now*. If you haven't read it, you should. Within the pages a prophecy is found that has since come to fruition, evidencing Michael's solid understanding of politics and the independence sentiment in our province. *No Other Option* looks at the independence movement not just from a political standpoint but, more importantly, the human condition within. This book delivers a solid appreciation of not only why our province 'doesn't fit' in Confederation but why a growing number of us have had enough and want out. Separatist or not, this is our history and a must read for every Albertan.

Kathy Flett, Board Director
Wildrose Independence Party of Alberta

Wagner is one of the few academics who can make eminent sense to the ordinary Joe.

Ted Byfield, Founder, *Alberta Report* magazine

Against the sentiments of a significant number of Albertans, the so-called Fair Deal Panel that Premier Jason Kenney appointed in 2019 refused to entertain independence as an option to redress the lopsided structures that disadvantage Alberta inside Canada. In this book, *No Other Option*, Michael Wagner boldly thrusts the argument for an independent Alberta back into the public square. Wagner pushes beyond constitution and economics. He re-articulates the central place of a unique and robust Alberta culture forged in the homesteading experiences that birthed it. Wagner's contribution enriches a debate all Albertans ought to contend with carefully, whether in agreement or in refusal. Alberta's thriving future rests on how Albertans will decide to deal with the unsustainable status quo, and no legitimate government should ever refuse considering any possible avenue to improve the lot of its people. This is a book for any citizen who, rejecting political taboos, favours open and constructive debate in a free society instead of informal suppression, and for all who want better for Alberta, regardless of the path preferred.

Dr. Marco Navarro-Génie, President
Haultain Research Institute

Contents Copyright © Michael Wagner, 2021
Cover Design & Illustration Copyright © Jeff Rout, 2021

Written by: Michael Wagner
Foreword by: Vince Byfield
Edited by: Jeff Rout

Published under license from Copyright owners.

All rights reserved. No part of this book may be reproduced in any form by an electronic or mechanical means, including information storage and retrieval systems, without permission in writing from the publisher, except by a reviewer who may quote brief passages in a review.

First Edition Paperback June 2021

ISBN 978-1-7775047-1-7

Published by Domino Effect Publishing, All Rights Reserved

No Other Option

Self-Determination for Alberta

By Michael Wagner

With foreword by Vince Byfield

To Danny Hozack,

a true champion of Alberta.

Michael Wagner

Table of Contents

FOREWORD

By Vince Byfield

Caution: for Albertans this book, once read, cannot be "un-read."
Its words may burn in their bellies for the rest of their days and
quenchable only by the righting of the many wrongs Author Wagner
describes. It's the sort of fire that has been known to fuel the forging
of nations.

Wagner has assembled the most concise summary I have ever read on
the political grievances Albertans have been experiencing for the past
five generations. Those who double-check his research will likely
conclude his chronicling of the steady growth of Alberta separatist
sentiment to be accurate and fair.

The total sum of money that's now been "transferred" from Albertans
to Ottawa is a staggering $600 billion, which works out to well over
half a million dollars from every family. Were a man to be caught
robbing $500,000 from a single family he would be convicted of
grand theft larceny and thrown in jail. But when Ottawa takes that
much from every single home in the entire province it's called
"equalization" and the government doesn't get punished; it gets re-
elected.

This next generation of Albertans essentially has two options: do
we clean up this economic and political mess or do we leave it for
our kids to fix. The problem isn't going away. In fact, as Wagner
describes, it's getting worse.

I hail from the last generation that ultimately achieved nothing, but
not for lack of effort. Wagner describes our efforts in Chapter One.
We tried to work from within and to change our political system for
the better. We advocated for a reformed Senate as a way to more
fairly represent the very real regional differences within Canada. We
negotiated and secured what we believed to be solid amendments to
Canada's constitution that would forever protect provincial resources
from federal taxation.

But recent events have revealed to us that those constitutional guarantees are not worth the paper they are printed on and that the Supreme Court of Canada will simply ignore them. In the end, every effort our generation has made to rectify the problem has been thwarted. We tried to work within the system and we failed. We in the West wanted in but Ottawa, in no uncertain terms, has kicked us out. This is a bitter pill for our generation to swallow. Now it is up to this next generation to work from outside the system.

We did establish one thing however, and that is our adversary cannot be trusted. Whatever agreements we negotiated they have always found some legal loophole to get what they want, usually our hard-earned savings. Albertans today are free to ignore this painful lesson, as we chose to ignore those who warned us, but do so at their peril.

Alberta independence is inevitable. As the generation before tried in vain to show the rest of Canada, the current political structure is unsustainable. Efforts to fix the problem thus far have essentially band-aided fundamental systemic flaws. Albertans have to muster up the courage to rip the bandage off and start over. Whether this is the generation to do what must be done remains to be seen.

Wagner describes one ray of light. We are not alone. Remember, this material once read cannot be un-read. With each generation comes a fresh new wave of injustices, and those who reach the conclusion that sovereignty is the only answer seldom if ever change their mind. That's why separatist sentiment continues to steadily grow. It may ebb and flow inversely with the price of our resources, but overall the number of independence-minded Albertans has typically doubled after each new Ottawa outrage.

We now stand at a pivotal juncture. At least one in three in the province now desire some sort of sovereignty. Will that third be able to sway the remaining two-thirds that sovereignty is our only hope? The full consequences of this most recent Supreme Court of Canada loss are now taking root in the minds of Albertans as we speak.

Therefore, this could be the generation that finally tilts the balance towards sovereignty and finds a way out of this mess. Contrary to fear mongering there is ample evidence that the path to sovereignty will be both peaceful and prosperous.

It's possible you are reading these words right now because a friend or neighbour has asked you to consider joining the cause. Please take this consideration seriously for much is at stake.

Vince Byfield
Albertan

PREFACE

In 2009, I wrote a book on the history of Alberta separatism entitled, *Alberta: Separatism Then and Now*. At that time, Stephen Harper was prime minister and the separatist movement was at a low point. Harper was from Alberta and had been a key person in the early years of the Reform Party of Canada, so he was trusted by Albertans to protect their province from harmful federal policies.

In that book, I suggested that once Stephen Harper was no longer prime minister, the Alberta separatist movement would revive. With the election of Justin Trudeau in 2015, that prediction came to pass. It didn't take long for numerous Facebook groups promoting Western separatism to appear and gather members.

Still, the effect of Trudeau's anti-fossil fuel climate change policies took time to become clear and to alarm most Albertans. The Northern Gateway pipeline was permanently halted in November 2016, and the Energy East pipeline was cancelled in October 2017 due to regulatory changes. Bill C-69, the "no more pipelines" bill, as well as Bill C-48, the tanker ban that prevents Alberta oil exports from the Pacific coast, were passed in 2019.

By 2018, I was gathering materials on the West's history and politics to write pro-separatist articles for the internet. I could see that a new book advocating Alberta independence was necessary, but I was hesitant to write one due to the time commitment and energy it would involve.

During 2019, with Trudeau's anti-Alberta policies becoming ever more harmful, interest in *Alberta: Separatism Then and Now* began to develop for the first time. Thanks to the kindness of Peter Downing, I was invited to sell copies of the book at Wexit meetings in different parts of Alberta. Some people asked me if I was going to update it. I suggested instead that I might write an altogether new book and so I have.

This book is very different from *Alberta: Separatism Then and Now*. That one is a history of Alberta separatism up to 2008, whereas this one is an argument that Alberta should become independent. I hope they make a good pair.

There's a terminology issue that must be addressed. From the late 1960s until recently, the word used to describe the movement for Alberta independence was "separatism," and its supporters were "separatists." For most people, it's a familiar way of speaking about these matters. Due to this widespread usage, I am personally comfortable using those terms. However, these days some people consider the terms "separatist" and "separatism" to be pejorative. They prefer terms like "sovereigntist," "independence," and "secessionist."

I don't like the term "sovereigntist" because it seems rather vague, but "independence," "secessionism," and "secessionist" seem clear enough. Therefore, I use the terms "separatism" and "secessionism," as well as "separatist" and "secessionist" interchangeably. The goal of the movement described by these terms is "independence," that is, Alberta would become its own country.

INTRODUCTION

Alberta is rich in fossil fuels, which are essential components for advanced modern economies. With the energy crisis of the 1970s, Central Canada benefited enormously from Alberta's abundance through government-imposed low oil prices and an export tax on oil. Subsequently, as Alberta's oil was later allowed to reach world price levels, the federal government continued to reap large financial rewards at Alberta's expense.

Now, many voters in Central Canada want Alberta's fossil fuels to be locked in the ground, supposedly to prevent climate change. What this would mean for Albertans is crystal clear: poverty and a future without economic hope. In effect, Central Canada wants Alberta to return to its status of a have-not province, like it was before the discovery of oil at Leduc in 1947. To see the future that voters in Toronto and Montreal envision for Alberta, simply look back to the economic struggles the province experienced in its first few decades. It's not a pretty picture.

But there is absolutely no reason why Albertans should accept this fate. Albertans have the opportunity to determine their own future, and they should do so. Through entirely peaceful, legal, and constitutional means, Albertans have the power to choose a future of self-determination and prosperity. That is, Alberta can become an independent country.

Seceding from Canada to form an independent country is certainly a drastic step. But there is really no other option. Serious proposals have been made in the past to reform Canada so that the West could receive a greater voice in national institutions. These kinds of reforms—with the Triple-E Senate being top of the list—have been rejected and are no longer viable. This means that Albertans face a stark choice between the status quo, with its inevitable economic decline, or independence.

Many people in Alberta are very hesitant to embrace secession due to strong personal and emotional ties to Canada. This is reasonable and completely understandable. There is much that is laudable about Canada, including the freedom and prosperity it offers to its citizens. Canadians also have much to be proud of in their past, such as the courageous exploits of the Canadian military in the world wars as well as other conflicts. Indeed, there is much to admire about Canada when it is compared to the other countries of the world.

Nevertheless, Canada has been going in a rather unhappy direction since the late 1960s. Prime Minister Pierre Trudeau had a vision for a different kind of country that he did much to accomplish. It's not a coincidence that the first efforts to create a separatist organization in Alberta took place during Trudeau's first term as prime minister. Today, Pierre's son Justin pursues a different set of policies that harm Alberta's future.

There is a lesson to be drawn from these two periods of Trudeau administrations: If Albertans don't choose a new direction for their province, they will forever be entangled in cyclical periods of hostile federal policies.

Building a society on Alberta values

Since the 1970s, some very thoughtful and intelligent people have expressed concerns about Alberta's future within Canada. Beginning in the 1980s, one such person was Stephen Harper, the future prime minister. He was so concerned, in fact, that he helped to form and build the Reform Party of Canada, which was initially created to provide a voice for the West within the Canadian Parliament.

Unfortunately, as the Reform Party grew, the original Western emphasis of the party became eclipsed by the desire to elect a national government. Its purpose changed as it became a vehicle aimed at forming a conservative government in Ottawa, ultimately emerging as the Canadian Alliance in 2000 with Stockwell Day as leader. However, even as an aspiring pan-Canadian party (whether in its Reform or

Canadian Alliance mode), in Central Canada it was widely viewed as a Western party.

The Western nature of the party drew derogatory comments indicative of the attitudes of Central Canada. During the 2000 federal election, Liberal prime minister Jean Chrétien said, "I like to do politics with people from the East. Joe Clark and Stockwell Day are from Alberta. They are a different type. I'm joking. I'm serious" (Johnson 2006, 283).

Chrétien's comment clearly indicated that he believed Albertans were somehow different from Eastern Canadians, and not in a good way.

The results of the 2000 election were very disappointing to most Westerners because so many of them had voted for the Canadian Alliance. The Canadian Alliance elected 66 MPs, but only 2 were from ridings east of Manitoba.

In the aftermath of that election, Stephen Harper made the following perceptive observation:

> Alberta and much of the rest of Canada have embarked on divergent and potentially hostile paths to defining their country. Alberta has opted for the best of Canada's heritage – a combination of American enterprise and individualism with the British traditions of order and co-operation. We have created an open, dynamic, and prosperous society in spite of a continuously hostile federal government. Canada appears content to become a second-tier socialistic country, boasting ever more loudly about its economy and social services to mask its second-rate status, led by a second-world strongman appropriately suited for the task (Johnson 2006, 282).

Clearly, he saw Alberta and Canada as travelling along very different trajectories.

In light of these divergent paths, Harper made the following suggestion: "Westerners, but especially Albertans, founded the

Reform/Alliance to get 'in' to Canada. The rest of the country has responded by telling us in no uncertain terms that we do not share their 'Canadian values.' Fine. Let us build a society on Alberta values" (Johnson 2006, 284).

It was with this in mind that Harper contributed to the well-known "Firewall" letter, an open letter to Premier Ralph Klein that was published in the *National Post* in January 2001. Along with a few others, including some prominent University of Calgary political scientists, Harper proposed that Alberta maximize the use of its constitutional powers, such as creating its own pension plan and police force.

Stephen Harper was never a separatist and he would undoubtedly repudiate secession. He simply wanted Alberta to exercise more of its constitutional powers for the benefit of Albertans.

Nevertheless, anyone with a secessionist inclination could easily find inspiration from his words. Indeed, Harper's analysis lends itself to such an interpretation. If the situation was as bad as he says, then establishing an independent Alberta seems to be the most logical solution. In a sense, his comments about Alberta's situation in the wake of the 2000 federal election provide a concise summary of the case for Alberta independence.

As Harper suggested, Alberta and Canada have been going in different directions for a long time. This divergence reached a tipping point during Prime Minister Pierre Trudeau's first term in power. Before then, Alberta had been too poor economically to even consider leaving Canada. As well, the patriotic and emotional bonds with the rest of Canada were too strong to think about the independence option.

Then the situation began to change, in large part due to Pierre Trudeau. Alberta's energy resources became an increasingly significant economic asset, especially as a result of the energy crisis of the 1970s. The wealth generated by Alberta's oil and gas industry made the province an economic powerhouse that would be able to prosper as an independent country. Trudeau, of course, saw the oil wealth as a treasure that Alberta could be forced to share with the rest of Canada.

At the same time, Trudeau was remodeling the country, first with the Official Languages Act in 1969 to make Canada an officially bilingual country, and later with the constitutional changes of 1982. For many Westerners, these sorts of fundamental modifications reduced their affection for a country that was changing beneath their feet.

Structure of the book

The first chapter of this book looks at the fact that Westerners have long wanted to be full partners in Confederation. The Reform Party of Canada's original slogan, "The West Wants In," concisely and accurately summarized popular Western sentiment. The West felt "left out" of national decision-making, but rather than walking away, it wanted to get "in." Proposals for getting "in" were made by prominent Westerners, but Central Canada has always rejected the West's proposed solutions.

The second chapter looks at how Pierre Trudeau created Alberta separatism. He enacted very severe and discriminatory policies for the purpose of transferring Alberta's oil wealth to Central Canada. Fossil fuels are non-renewable resources, so they will eventually run out. If the wealth they generate is siphoned away, it cannot be used to diversify the economy and prepare Alberta for the future. Therefore, the loss of wealth harmed Alberta for the long-term. This was one of Pierre Trudeau's legacies – long-term damage to Alberta's economy.

Pierre Trudeau is the father of Alberta separatism. His policies generated the Alberta separatist movement and increased support for its goals. Survey data indicate support for Alberta independence was in the single-digit range before 1980, but has remained in the double-digit range ever since.

The third chapter briefly describes the crisis that Alberta faces due to the current federal government and the policies favoured by Central Canada. Alberta is being harmed in two major ways. On the one hand, large amounts of Alberta's wealth have been siphoned off by the federal government to be distributed to other provinces, especially

Quebec. And on the other hand, Central Canada is dead-set on shutting down Alberta's oil and gas industry – the very industry that generates the wealth. The only way Alberta can escape these injustices is by becoming independent.

The fourth chapter looks at how Alberta is in some respects historically and culturally different from the rest of the country. Although economic issues have always been at the core of Albertans' anger towards the federal government, a sense of Alberta identity is necessary to build a new country.

That is, if the desire for independence is based exclusively on economic considerations (as it largely has been so far), it will only last until those economic circumstances change. Loyalty to a country should not be based on financial considerations alone. In such a case, it would seem, one's patriotism simply goes to the highest bidder. Loyalty to Alberta should be much more firmly grounded than that, and the province's unique historical and cultural traits provide a basis for an authentic Alberta identity.

The fifth chapter will consider whether the Conservative Party of Canada provides a viable solution to Alberta's predicament, as so many people presume. The answer is No. The CPC is motivated by many of the same considerations as the Liberal Party of Canada and will always have the incentive to ignore Western interests to win Central Canadian votes.

The sixth chapter will explain that a legal avenue to Alberta independence is available. In 1998, the Supreme Court of Canada created a constitutional pathway for provincial secession, so Alberta can legally and peacefully achieve independence.

The seventh chapter provides a brief account of recent developments in Alberta's independence movement.

So that's it. Albertans can, and should, choose the prosperous future for themselves and their children that is only available through independence and self-determination.

Chapter 1

THE WEST WANTED IN

For generations, Westerners have manifested a trait that came to be known as "Western alienation." Essentially, since the early days of Prairie settlement, Westerners have been unhappy with the political and economic treatment they received from Central Canada and the federal government.

In 1970, at a conference in Lethbridge, Alberta premier Harry Strom said the following:

> The issue of Alberta's place in Confederation has been subject to lively debate throughout our history. With the other Prairie provinces we have shared in a number of political movements which expressed our discontent with powerlessness in the face of Quebec votes and Ontario manufacturers.

> We have always had a sense of economic exploitation. This notion has marked all political parties in the West. The cartoon that has captured these sentiments is the one of a large cow standing on a map of Canada munching grass in Alberta and Saskatchewan with milk pouring from a bulging udder into the large buckets in Ontario.

> To some degree this problem is one of our own perceptions or feelings of insecurity. But there is also a basis for our resentment—we have felt that the West was opened to settlement to line the pockets of eastern pot and pan salesmen (Strom 1970, 32).

This was said over 50 years ago, and Premier Strom was reflecting on previous decades of disenchantment. He also pointed out that, "At the heart of this issue are those aspirations and concerns of Alberta people which require recognition and action at the federal level if they are to be realized" (Strom 1970, 32). The situation has only gotten worse since he spoke those words, so long ago.

Ernest Manning's proposal for Senate reform

During the course of the 1970s, conflict between Alberta and the federal government intensified like never before. War in the Middle East in 1973 led to a dramatic spike in the price of oil. Rather than allow Alberta to benefit from its oil resources, Prime Minister Pierre Trudeau decided to impose an export tax on oil and keep the price of Alberta's oil low for Central Canada. Alberta premier Peter Lougheed fought back hard against these measures, but the federal government had the upper hand.

Eventually, especially after Trudeau imposed the National Energy Program (NEP) in 1980, many Albertans began to question whether the West would be better off as an independent country. Others, however, thought reasonable reforms could be enacted to protect the interests of Alberta within Confederation.

Among these were University of Lethbridge political scientist Peter McCormick, Senator Ernest C. Manning (premier of Alberta from 1943-1968), and former British Columbia MLA Gordon Gibson. In 1981 they wrote a report for the Canada West Foundation proposing Senate reform entitled, *Regional Representation: The Canadian Partnership*. They argued that Western alienation was a chronic problem that needed to be addressed:

> "Western alienation", like the other manifestations of Canadian regionalism, is not a transient epiphenomenon of Canadian politics that will go away if we somehow manage to outwait it. Instead, it is the most recent outbreak of a condition that has been chronic in this country since Confederation, not just in the West but in other parts of Canada as well, and all reasonable expectations are that it will continue to be chronic in the future. Underlying conditions of a broad-based nature generate regionalism in Canada; constitutional flaws and deficiencies

continually function as catalysts to impel this potential toward overt manifestation. Although any one of these outbursts may be short-lived, the overall pattern is not. Canada has muddled through until now but there is no guarantee that this luck will last indefinitely (McCormick, Manning, and Gibson 1981, 3).

They explained that institutional reforms to improve regional representation were necessary if Canada was to avoid the possibility of Western provinces moving towards independence:

In an age of self-determination and democratic self-government, it can never be illegitimate for a group of people to consider the possible costs and benefits of reorganization into a smaller nation state. Our perpetual inferiority complex vis-a-vis our huge southern neighbor should not blind us to the fact that many countries much smaller in area and population than Canada exist and prosper, nor is there any strong correlation between size and economic well-being. It may or may not be the case that separation and independence for any part of Canada are undesirable, and that the gains would not off-set the costs, but it remains legitimate to raise the possibility that any one region might be so ill-served by Confederation as to benefit from leaving. An effective system of regional representation, perceived so by the inhabitants of all regions, would go far toward ensuring that such a debate would always be resolved in favor of Canada (McCormick, Manning, and Gibson 1981, 10).

Their central argument was that Canada needed to choose between such institutional reform and the possible secession of the West from Canada:

The choice is not whether Canada shall have or not have strong regional loyalties; history has already made that choice for us. Rather, the choice is whether such forces shall be channelled and accommodated by providing them with an effective focus within the institutions of national government, or whether our national institutional arrangements will largely ignore federalism, leave provincial governments as the only credible focus for regional concerns, and flirt with the possibility of the extreme manifestation of frustrated regionalism—separatism (McCormick, Manning, and Gibson 1981, 134-135).

This was written forty years ago. It is just as true today, and even more imperative.

David Kilgour's Uneasy Patriots

Seven years later, in 1988, David Kilgour, a Progressive Conservative MP from Edmonton, wrote the book, *Uneasy Patriots: Western Canadians in Confederation*. In this book, he explored the history and basis of Western alienation, and called for reforms to make the West a full and equal partner within Canada.

Kilgour summarized the reasons for Western alienation as follows:

> Western Canada's past and present disenchantment is based on both economic and philosophical grounds. The classic elements of Western discontent formed the fabric of its political life and were the greatest impediment to the development of its full potential: the concentration of economic and political power in Central Canada, the lack of an effective regional banking system, the disadvantage to western consumers resulting from protective tariffs on imported goods, the lack of a national freight rate policy that permits western goods to compete in eastern markets, inequality in federal procurement and development funds, and the lack of a comprehensive development policy at the federal level which would lead to decentralization and equitable distribution of economic opportunity (Kilgour 1988, 251).

In the face of these disadvantages, Westerners did not sit back and do nothing. As Kilgour explained, "History shows that Westerners have attempted within the framework of existing institutions to make our voices heard in Ottawa, yet have failed to achieve political and economic equality with Central Canada. Western alienation is, alas, alive and well" (Kilgour 1988, 262).

The problems underlying Western alienation were ongoing and needed a solution. What was the solution? "Major institutional changes are clearly required, but the major obstacle is probably the ongoing indifference of government and private sector policy-makers in Central Canada. Westerners seek major changes on both the attitudinal and institutional fronts" (Kilgour 1988, 262).

Kilgour concluded that, "The time has come to address a long-standing injustice and bring the West into equal partnership with all other regions of the country. Political, economic and cultural equality is the means of ending western alienation" (Kilgour 1988, 263).

Yes, by 1988 "the time had come" to address the "long-standing injustice" experienced by the West. That was over thirty years ago, and the situation is the same (or worse) today.

This is the key point here. Premier Strom talked about the problem in 1970. Prof. Peter McCormick, Senator Ernest C. Manning and Gordon Gibson wrote about the problem and proposed a meaningful solution in 1981. David Kilgour also wrote about the problem and the need for solutions in 1988. These men were all mainstream political leaders representing a large proportion of Albertans.

Westerners have been trying to reform the country for decades and they have little to show for their efforts. That doesn't mean their efforts were inept or not worthwhile. Quite to the contrary. Trying to reform the country was the right thing to do. It was the reasonable thing to do. But over the course of decades, Westerners learned that the deck was stacked against them.

The evolution of Western discontent

Westerners have had complaints against the East going back to the earliest years of settlement. Indeed, Louis Riel led rebellions against the federal government twice, in 1869-70 and 1885. Later, farmers would create political organizations to represent their views to Ottawa. The Progressive Party of Canada was very popular in the West and elected a number of MPs from the region during the 1920s. Subsequent iterations of Western political dissent, such as Social Credit and the Reform Party of Canada are well-known.

Despite the seeming consistency of Western dissatisfaction for over a century, something important did change in the West's perception of Canada. Westerners' understanding of the cause of their plight has evolved over time. In the earlier period before the Second World War, they believed the source of their problems lay in sinister organizations or in the economic system itself. Complaints against the Canadian Pacific Railway (CPR) and Eastern bankers are legendary. The Social Credit Party wanted to reform the monetary system, whereas the Co-operative Commonwealth Federation (CCF) saw capitalism itself as the problem.

However, as University of Alberta historian Doug Owram explains, Westerners subsequently began to realize that their problems were rooted in the structure of Confederation itself, not in particular organizations or the economic system.

As Owram put it,

> Until the 1930s, western political protest tended to focus on either political structures or, more often, on "special interests." These special interests, whether banks, railway companies, or whatever, were perceived as using their power and their influence to affect national policy in their favour and against the interests of the West. The political response, therefore, tended to be framed in terms of reform. Programs to nationalize the CPR, reform the monetary system, smash the bankers, control the Grain Exchange, or whatever, all concentrated on attacks on systems thwarting the functioning of democracy. Reform of the system was the answer to western grievance because once the reforms were instituted, the grievances would disappear (Owram 1981, 58).

After World War Two, however, Westerners began to perceive that the problem was much more fundamental than they originally understood. The problem was the structure of Confederation itself:

> Regional self-interests do differ and that fact leads to different expectations not just among elites but among the average voter as well. The real threat to the West, this chain of argument goes, comes from the consumer and worker in central Canada. The essential problem is not the money system or capitalism

but the nature of democracy itself and especially the age-old problem of what has been termed the "tyranny of the majority" (Owram 1981, 58).

In other words, because Ontario and Quebec contain well over 50 percent of Canada's population, Central Canada controls the federal government. That means the federal government will always enact policies in the best interest of Central Canada, not the West. This is a feature of the system, not a bug. As Westerners see things, Canadian politics are "designed to keep the region in a subordinate position relative to Ontario and Quebec. The West has never felt in control of its own destiny" (Owram 1981, 61).

Besides gaining a more accurate perception of the cause of the problem, there is one other way that things have changed for the West. Unlike the first half of the twentieth century, the West is now economically prosperous and would be able to survive on its own. As Owram wrote,

> The West was, in its early days, too much a frontier region to consider going it alone and then, through the 1930s and for a time after, too poor to make such an option worth considering. The new wealth of the region has changed this and many Westerners, especially in Alberta, believe that being part of Canada imposes a financial obstacle to the West's further prosperity (Owram 1981, 61-62).

In other words, while being a part of Canada may have been economically beneficial for the West during its first few decades, this is no longer the case. The kinds of policies now being imposed upon the West (e.g., Bill C-69 and Bill C-48) mean that an independent West would clearly be more prosperous. The economic case for remaining in Canada has evaporated.

Why does this matter? Because the two changes described here help to highlight the case for Western independence. First of all, early Western political activists had not fully recognized that the structure of Confederation was itself the root of the West's problems, and therefore thought that certain reforms would be enough to solve their problems. Their proposed reforms were insufficient. Later generations, however, saw more clearly that Central Canadian dominance was systemic. This realization means that the West's problems cannot be solved within Canada.

Secondly, the early West wasn't strong enough economically to go it alone. Now it is more than strong enough to survive on its own.

Of course, one obvious solution to the West's situation within Canada would be constitutional reform. Improving representational institutions, especially the Senate, could provide the West with the clout that it needs to prevent anti-Western policies from being pursued by the federal government.

There were, in fact, constitutional changes made in 1982, and some of the changes were beneficial to the Western provinces. But, unfortunately, the kind of change that would have addressed the West's representational concerns was ignored.

The 1982 Constitution

In 1982 Canada underwent a significant constitutional transformation. For decades, the provincial and federal governments had discussed the need for changes in the Constitution, but agreement on those changes was out of reach. However, during the 1980 Quebec sovereignty referendum campaign, Prime Minister Pierre Trudeau promised Quebecers that he would push for constitutional alterations.

Trudeau was successful in fulfilling that promise. Canada got the *Constitution Act, 1982*. Most importantly, it added a *Charter of Rights and Freedoms* and an amending formula so that Canada could revise its own constitution without input from the British Parliament. There were also a few other modifications.

For the West, there was a positive side and a negative side. On the one hand, provincial control of non-renewable natural resources was made more explicit. But on the other hand, institutional changes that could have improved the West's position within Canada were ignored.

As University of Calgary political scientist Roger Gibbins has written, the Alberta government's constitutional objectives during the negotiations were primarily defensive. That is, the top priority was protecting Alberta's ownership and control of resources from the federal government. This strategy was successful – Section 92(A) was added to the Constitution, thus clarifying and protecting the province's resource ownership. Such protection was particularly important in light of Pierre Trudeau's desire to seize Alberta's oil wealth.

Alberta was also successful in helping to draft the amending formulae for the Constitution. As Gibbins wrote,

> It was here that the government made substantial progress with respect not only to the protection of provincial resources, but also with respect to the *constitutional enshrinement of provincial equality*. The general amending formula in section 38 (1) – Parliament plus seven of the ten provinces having in aggregate at least fifty per cent of the population of all provinces – recognizes the equality of the provinces by denying any single province the power of veto (Gibbins 1992, 73).

In short, the Alberta government was justified in seeing the 1982 constitutional changes in a positive light due to protections for Alberta's resources and a recognition of provincial equality. However, as Gibbins added, "the defensive posture of the provincial government also meant that no progress was made with respect to the reform of national parliamentary institutions" (Gibbins 1992, 74).

Such lack of reform in national institutions was the subject of one of Gibbins' earlier articles. As he explained, the kinds of institutional reforms that could have improved the West's place within Canada were entirely neglected:

> In the end, the constitutional Accord failed to address, much less solve, the chronic problems of regional representation that have fostered western alienation and eroded the bond between western Canadians and their national government. The opportunity to fulfill the long-standing desire of western Canadians to be full partners in Confederation was lost when institutional reform was abandoned, and the blame must be shared by both levels of government (Gibbins 1983, 122).

During the constitutional negotiations of the early 1980s, many Albertans were dead-set against Trudeau's proposals. He had poisoned the well by introducing the National Energy Program (NEP) which involved a full-scale attack on Alberta's oil industry. How could Albertans have any confidence in Trudeau's constitutional agenda when he was trying to steal the source of their prosperity?

As Gibbins pointed out,

> in Alberta, the immensely unpopular NEP and the constitutional proposals were commonly seen as a single package. Public meetings held to discuss the constitutional proposals focused almost entirely on the NEP, and the NEP became the layman's interpretive guide to the constitution debate. The Constitution Act proposals were seen as a means to constitutionally entrench the NEP, while the NEP was seen to foreshadow the dangers ahead should the Constitution Act become the law of the land (Gibbins 1983, 124).

Of course, the blame for all of this falls squarely on Pierre Trudeau.

> Ottawa's initial constitutional proposals contained nothing to appeal to western Canadians *as western Canadians*. There was no rhetorical appeal to western visions of the national community, no attempt to address western resource and transportation concerns or western fears surrounding the declaratory, emergency, reservation and spending powers of the federal government. There was no implicit constitutional log-rolling, no regional trade-off of constitutional costs and benefits. In the West, as a consequence, constitution-making was not an exercise in nation-building; Ottawa's proposals were seen by far too many western Canadians as the regionally-insensitive product of one government, one party, and one man (Gibbins 1983, 125).

Gibbins noted that in the past, Westerners had a strong national vision. Yet, today, this truly national vision has been largely eroded.

In the past, western Canadians have had a strong national vision. They, after all, were the Canadian nation-builders; they were the people from foreign lands who merged with and fostered a new Canadian nationality, who broke the prairie sod and pushed back the resource frontier, who participated enthusiastically in the two world wars that did so much to define Canadian nationhood. Admittedly, the western national vision was not always well-suited to broader political realities; John Diefenbaker's "one Canada" had little appeal to the nation's francophones, and western support for Canada's war efforts was tinged with hostility towards Quebec. Nevertheless, there was in the West a truly *national* vision, which today has begun to falter and fade. The "national interest" is spoken of with derisive cynicism, and for many the "national" government is not only remote from, but apart from the West. The Constitution Act, with its understandable, if regrettable lack of rhetorical flourishes, does nothing to revive the national vision in the West. There is no emotional linkage to the strong sense of Canadian nationalism that used to be so prevalent in the region (Gibbins 1983, 130).

Trudeau's constitutional changes did nothing to address the West's cynicism. Aside from clearer protections for natural resources, the West's historic complaints about the unfair structure of Confederation were ignored. Instead of a national vision, the constitutional changes entrenched Pierre Trudeau's vision for Canada.

Gibbins explained that Alberta has tried to get Canada to implement institutional reforms, but these efforts have been rebuffed:

From the early institutional radicalism of the United Farmers of Alberta and the economic radicalism of Social Credit through the Senate reformers of the last decade and the Reform Party of Canada, Albertans have again and again challenged the constitutional and institutional organization of Canadian political life. What is striking, however, is that the Alberta challenge has had little if any impact on the national scene. The national preoccupation with Quebec has been so pervasive and so complete that Alberta initiatives for *institutional reform* have gone all but unnoticed (Gibbins 1992, 81).

Among Alberta's initiatives was an election in October, 1989 to select someone that Premier Don Getty could recommend to Prime Minister Brian Mulroney for appointment to the Senate. Reform Party candidate Stan Waters won the election and was, in fact, appointed to the Senate. But this did not lead to the anticipated change. As Gibbins explained, "At the time, there was a strong expectation among Senate reformers that the Alberta election would set into motion similar elections across the country, and that Alberta would lead the country towards substantive Senate reform. In fact, nothing happened, or at least has happened to date" (Gibbins 1992, 82).

The hopeless task of reforming Canada

Most Westerners are still patriotic Canadians who want the country to work. They're willing to give Canada one more chance to rectify the injustices against the West. Constitutional reform is still often suggested as a way to achieve this goal.

However, there is a problem with the argument for trying to reform Canada: over the last forty years or so, many good people have been trying to bring about such reforms and they haven't gotten anywhere. If those people weren't able to achieve the kinds of changes necessary to get a fair deal for the West, what makes others think they could achieve them now?

To state this point most bluntly: if Preston Manning and the Reform Party of Canada were unable to make the kinds of changes Western Canada needs, then it can't be done.

The Reform Party was the West's best chance of getting a better deal within Canada. Many of the region's top people were involved. Thousands of well-meaning Westerners put all kinds of time and money into getting the party off the ground and sustaining it for several years. It was the dominant federal party in Alberta until it folded into the Canadian Alliance. There is nothing like it in Western politics today, and even if all of the groups calling for constitutional reform were amalgamated, their efforts would look miniscule beside the old Reform Party.

In a book chronicling the initial rise of the Reform Party, Ted Byfield described the historical injustices done to the West, making a new party necessary. As he pointed out, during the Liberal government of Prime Minister Pierre Trudeau, it increasingly "began to look as though Canada was a mere con game, being played out by Ontario and Quebec at the expense of the West" (Byfield 1991a, 3).

But instead of turning to independence, most Westerners at that time just wanted fairness within Canada. So, with the Reform Party, "No longer would the West talk about 'getting out of Canada.' Instead the slogan became, 'The West Wants In,' a phrase coined by *Alberta Report* columnist Ralph Hedlin. It means that the West wants constitutional changes that will enable it to play a more equal role in Canadian affairs, notably a Triple-E Senate" (Byfield 1991a, 5).

The Reform Party made a tremendous effort, but fundamental problems remain.

The fact is that fighting for a better deal for the West within Canada has been going on, in one form or another, for decades. Besides the Reform Party, there were various other advocates for Senate reform at least since the early 1980s. Especially noteworthy is Bert Brown and his Canadian Committee for a Triple-E Senate.

But despite such great efforts, their goal was never achieved.

These people should be applauded for their efforts. It makes perfect sense to advocate reform before proposing more drastic solutions. But they worked hard, did their very best, and central Canada offered them what central Canada will always offer discontented Westerners – nothing.

Does anyone really think that a new Western political movement can be organized that could equal the Reform Party, let alone improve on its achievements? Because that, at minimum, is what it's going to take to accomplish the kinds of changes necessary for the West to get a fair deal.

In short, over the years there have been plenty of proposals and attempts to improve the situation of the West within Canada. They

have all failed for the same reason – Central Canada is not interested.
Central Canada is completely satisfied with the status quo and
knows that the West is powerless to do anything about it within the
framework of Confederation.

Historical grievances before Pierre Trudeau

As must be clear by now, the West has had various complaints
about its treatment by Central Canada at least since the early
twentieth century. However, to be fair to Canada, not all of these
grievances necessarily provide a justifiable basis for secession. The
historical injustices are real, but the strongest arguments for Western
independence do not become clear until Pierre Trudeau became prime
minister.

University of Alberta economist Kenneth Norrie has argued that the
classic examples given of federal government discrimination against
the West are not as clear as many have supposed. From his analysis,
he concluded that arguments about the West's lack of economic
development, the higher prices it had to pay, and discriminatory
freight rates, were frequently explainable by the West's geography and
demography, rather than specific government policies.

As he wrote, "many of the Prairie grievances must be interpreted as
dissatisfaction with a market economy rather than with discriminatory
policies of the federal government" (Norrie 1979, 131). Furthermore,
"many of the apparently more legitimate arguments are incompletely
analyzed. Achievement of one goal may in fact prejudice the
attainment of others, or involve an income redistribution within the
Prairies that is not necessarily desirable" (Norrie 1979, 131). That is,
a policy that is harmful to one sector of the Prairie economy may, in
fact, be beneficial to another sector.

His analysis, then, suggests that certain classic arguments underlying
Western alienation were not as thoroughly supported by economic
reality as many Westerners would suppose.

However, that conclusion only applied to the West's economic
situation before the energy crisis of the 1970s. Under Pierre Trudeau,
the federal government did begin to actively discriminate against

the West. In particular, the policies he initiated to seize Alberta's oil wealth were clearly detrimental to the West.

Regarding Trudeau's energy policies, Norrie wrote,

> In general, the arguments of the western provinces are valid. Economic rents properly belong to the owners of the resources when ownership is public rather than private, and as such clearly should accrue in the first instance to the provincial governments. This fact, plus the long-standing tradition of one level of government not taxing another, means that the export tax on crude oil and the domestic price freeze are clearly regional burdens. There is a direct subsidy from the producing provinces to the federal government and to Canadian consumers of western oil to the extent of the difference between world and Canadian oil prices. The punitive features of this policy are even more apparent given that the federal government has not imposed similar measures on other types of products (Norrie 1979, 139).

Trudeau's energy policies – and remember, this was written *before* the National Energy Program – were "punitive" to the West and Alberta in particular. Norrie questioned the economic basis of Western alienation before the 1970s, but he noted a significant economic basis for it under Pierre Trudeau.

In 1981, Norrie and another University of Alberta economist, Michael Percy, wrote an article explaining the likely impact of Alberta's independence on its economy. Needless to say, an independent Alberta would reap enormous financial benefits from the sale of its oil and gas resources. However, they warn, the long-term impact of such heavy dependence on oil revenue could ultimately lead to negative economic consequences, largely because an over-dependence on the energy industry could result in the shrinkage of other industries and therefore a less diversified economy overall.

Of course, Norrie and Percy were opposed to Alberta secession and wrote their article to caution people not to view independence as such an economic boon as many would expect. Nevertheless, they were clear that the policies of the Trudeau government since the beginning of the energy crisis were problematic for Alberta:

> Are federal energy policies unfair to the West? If one accepts
> that the provinces own the resources and thus are entitled to
> control their development and determine the allocation of
> revenues derived from them, then they definitely are. The
> federal government has, since 1973, via a complex system
> of price controls, export taxes, and surcharges, appropriated
> a share of potential oil and gas revenues far in excess of
> what it takes from other sectors of the economy. This action
> appears to be especially unfair in that Ottawa has not moved
> to tax equivalently other types of energy products such as
> hydroelectricity where rents have arisen as a direct consequence
> of oil and gas price increases (Norrie and Percy 1981, 181).

They went on to explain that such discriminatory policies towards the
West quite reasonably led to people seeking a better future outside of
Canada:

> It is also easy to see how this asymmetric response has given
> rise to demands for political independence. The classic rationale
> for a federal form of government is that it protects minorities
> from the tyranny of the majority in instances where this might
> be expected to be consistently a problem. Eastern Canada with
> its concentration of population and hence votes is completely
> dependent on energy imports while the much smaller West is
> a significant net exporter. Thus, their interests will diverge and
> in any vote the energy-consuming regions will always prevail
> (Norrie and Percy 1981, 181).

Here, again, it is clear that Trudeau's policies unfairly targeted Alberta.
It was Trudeau who clarified the case for Alberta secession.

Conclusion

The West has long been dissatisfied with its place within Confederation.
This situation has given rise to what is commonly called "Western
alienation." Prominent people and organizations have proposed
solutions to the West's problems, but Central Canada is comfortable
with the existing arrangement and is not interested in helping the West.

Therefore, independence is the only remaining option for the West, and Alberta in particular.

Kenneth Norrie has argued that the economic validity of many historic Western complaints is ambiguous. However, he has also demonstrated that there is a much stronger basis for Western discontent beginning with Pierre Trudeau's energy policies in the 1970s. There is no ambiguity to the anti-Western and especially anti-Alberta nature and impact of those policies.

The next chapter picks up this line of thought to argue that it was Pierre Trudeau who first provided a genuine basis for Alberta independence.

Chapter 2

PIERRE TRUDEAU AND THE CHANGE HE WROUGHT

The purpose of this chapter is to argue that Prime Minister Pierre Trudeau provided the first legitimate basis for Alberta secessionism. As mentioned in the previous chapter, Alberta and the other Prairie provinces have had serious grievances with Canada since at least the early twentieth century. The nature of these grievances, though, fell short of providing a convincing case for independence.

However, Pierre Trudeau transformed the situation. He was different from other prime ministers in his willingness to use federal power to strip Alberta of the benefits of its resource wealth. No province had been plundered to such a degree before. Although this began in 1973, it reached its apex with the National Energy Program (NEP) in 1980.

Trudeau also achieved a significant alteration of the country through his constitutional changes of 1982. One purpose of his *Canadian Charter of Rights and Freedoms* was to create a new kind of Canadian identity at the expense of provincial identities. Trudeau hoped Canadians would develop a national bond that would supersede their loyalty to their province or region by viewing the *Charter* as the source of their rights.

It was shortly after Trudeau became prime minister that the first Alberta separatist organizations began to form. With Trudeau regaining power in 1980 and subsequently implementing the NEP, surveys reported a notable increase in support for Alberta independence. In short, Pierre Trudeau created a seismic shift that provided the impetus for Alberta secessionism.

This is not to say that the idea of an independent Alberta had never crossed anyone's mind before. Rather, what is meant is that there was no organized political expression of secessionism before Trudeau became prime minister. He created the conditions that for the first time led to political organizing with the purpose of attaining Alberta independence.

Canada has changed

There are a lot of good things that can be said about Canada, and Westerners have long been known as Canadian patriots. But much has changed in recent decades.

University of Calgary professors David Bercuson and Barry Cooper have written about Canada's decline in the latter part of the twentieth century. They explain the original purpose of Confederation, and how that purpose became subverted after World War Two, especially under the administration of Pierre Trudeau.

Bercuson and Cooper point out that the original colonies/provinces confederated in 1867 primarily for economic reasons. By uniting, they believed they could create a national government with the resources to build a country that would generate greater economic prosperity than each of the smaller units could do on their own. As Bercuson and Cooper explain,

> Only when the national government was able to marshal effectively the resources of the nation and to direct westward expansion, settlement, railway construction, and industrial development would the real aim of Confederation be achieved – namely, prosperity as a British Dominion. As long as that happened, the New Nationality would hold together out of self-interest and the mutual support of disparate groups in the common enterprise of what we now call nation building (Bercuson and Cooper 1994, 51).

This was the predominant view of federal leaders until the 1950s, and it did not begin to change until Prime Minister John Diefenbaker came to power. He saw Canada as more than an economic alliance but was unable to change the country in any notable way.

After Diefenbaker, however, Prime Minister Lester Pearson began
to take the country in a new direction. Pearson's government wanted
to establish what being a Canadian really meant. As Bercuson and
Cooper write,

> the new Canadian character itself was going to be created in
> the image of the thinkers and doers that Pearson had collected
> around him. So, for example, Canada was going to be bilingual
> and bicultural whether or not it made sense of Canadian
> reality, whether or not the nation could afford it, whether or
> not it actually drew Canadians together. They would do so
> by making bilingualism and biculturalism part of the national
> creed and, by lifting it above politics, turn it into an expression
> of our collective public virtue (Bercuson and Cooper 1994,
> 109).

This meant that by 1967 the role of the federal government had
changed significantly: "Henceforth that role was not simply to
administer, but to create and shape and mould a national character and,
above all, to pursue collective public virtue" (Bercuson and Cooper
1994, 112). Canada would henceforth be on a different path.

It was in this atmosphere that Pierre Trudeau entered politics and
became prime minister in 1968. Even more than his predecessor,
Trudeau wanted to substantially change the country of which he had
become leader.

There were two major components of Trudeau's agenda: "First, he
would make Canada the kind of place where Quebeckers would feel
at home anywhere. And second, he would make Canada, including
the now comfortable and well-adjusted Quebeckers, a just society. His
tool would be the state" (Bercuson and Cooper 1994, 124).

The bottom line of Trudeau's major policy initiatives and pursuit of
a "just society" all had one thing in common: "increased intervention
by the state in the operation of the economy and in the daily lives of
ordinary citizens" (Bercuson and Cooper 1994, 138-139).

Trudeau came to power facing a major challenge from the growth of
Quebec nationalism. Within a few years he was also faced with an
energy crisis due to the rapid rise of oil prices resulting from war in

the Middle East. After his come-back re-election victory of 1980, he decided to aggressively tackle both issues.

Bercuson and Cooper outline Trudeau's goals as follows:

> The logic was clear but never could be admitted: if Alberta's energy revenues could be appropriated by Ottawa, and then redirected by it, the economy would hum; if the constitution could be changed, Quebec would be happy to remain in Canada. Even if it proved impossible to change the constitution, the "redirection" of energy revenues as regional equalization payments held the promise of making Bourassa's profitable federalism attractive (Bercuson and Cooper 1994, 143-144).

The idea of "profitable federalism" was that Quebec should remain in Canada (rather than separate) because of the financial rewards it would receive, mostly as a result of Alberta's oil wealth.

Trudeau pushed through his constitutional changes but they did not satisfy Quebec. Nevertheless, those changes—and especially the adoption of the *Charter of Rights and Freedoms*—fundamentally altered Canada (Wagner 2012).

Besides his constitutional initiative, Trudeau unveiled his infamous National Energy Program (NEP). It was predicated on the belief that Alberta was benefiting too much from high oil prices. Why should a pipsqueak province like Alberta profit at the expense of Ontario and Quebec?

The NEP severely damaged Alberta's oil and gas industry. It was later repealed by the government of Prime Minister Brian Mulroney, although Mulroney's government itself favoured Central Canada over the West.

Pierre Trudeau and the development of Western separatism

The NEP brought enmity between Alberta and Pierre Trudeau to its height. However, Albertans' dislike for Trudeau had been growing for over ten years prior to the NEP.

In 1969, *The Toronto Telegram* newspaper undertook the Canada 70 study, which involved surveying the attitudes of citizens across the country. One of the products of this study was a book entitled, *The Prairie Provinces: Alienation and Anger* which was written by *The Telegram*'s Ottawa Bureau chief, Peter Thompson.

Much of the book is a sympathetic discussion of Western alienation and the reasons for it. Thompson sought out the views of many Westerners and seems to have obtained an authentic sense of their frustrations with Central Canada. This provides a basis for him to accurately explain a genuine Western perspective to his Toronto audience.

Early in the book, Thompson writes:

> Many Western Canadians are getting mad. They have been disenchanted for generations with the East over economic inequities because the best interest of the Western primary producer is fundamentally opposed to that of the Eastern manufacturer. They have been disturbed by their apparent inability to influence the political and financial decisions of the nation (Thompson 1969, 2).

In other words, "The real basis of Western discontent as Canada enters the 1970s is the fact that too many decisions guiding the Prairie destiny are made in Ottawa, Toronto, and Montreal" (Thompson 1969, 5).

Of course, in 1969 Canada had a rookie prime minister named Pierre Trudeau. The Canada 70 study was able to get a comment from Trudeau about discontent in Western Canada. He began by saying, "Perhaps, to be quite candid with you when you talk of growing disenchantment, I must begin by saying that some of my reading of the West is that it is always disenchanted" (Thompson 1969, 4). In other words, his basic assumption was that Westerners are a bunch of chronic whiners. His attitude towards the West was cynical from the start.

Perhaps not surprisingly, then, Thompson sensed the budding of secessionist sentiment in the West. Indeed, the concluding chapter of his book is entitled, "Seeds of Separation."

As he explains, the prairie West had been relatively poor from the early part of the twentieth century until the 1960s. During that decade, however, its economic situation began to improve, leading to new political thinking: "Not until the mid-1960s did the West halt to take stock, of both its riches and its position within Confederation. It found the riches to be vast in dollar value but apparently limited in power to change the industrial and social structures of Canada" (Thompson 1969, 73).

The result was that many Westerners became determined to get a better deal from Canada. As Thompson pointed out, "The suggestion implicit in the West's confident tone is that if this game is rigged," then "the West is getting out. The West is in a position to set some of the rules because it has more than its share of wealth in the game" (Thompson 1969, 73-74).

He quickly added that there were only "tiny seeds of separatist thought" in the West. However, he then pointed out that if the federal government does not deal fairly with the West, it "could force those tiny seeds of Western separatism into a growing movement within a decade" (Thompson 1969, 74).

Thompson's words were prophetic because the first serious secessionist organizations began to form in Alberta during the 1970s.

Thompson was able to interview Premier Harry Strom – the last Social Credit premier of Alberta – and asked him about Western sentiment. Strom's view was that "it would take a man of national stature to stir up the scattered separatist feeling in the West." Although he did not think such a leader was then on the horizon, "such men have been known to emerge almost overnight" (Thompson 1969, 74).

The main point to be made here is that early in Pierre Trudeau's first term in office, some Westerners began to seriously think about secession from Canada.

The first appearance of organized Alberta separatism

Not coincidentally, then, the first baby-steps in organizing the secessionist movement were made shortly after Pierre Trudeau took power.

Upon becoming prime minister in April, 1968, one of Trudeau's top priorities was the passage of the Official Languages bill. The purpose of the bill was to give French and English equal status in the government of Canada, with the idea that doing so would redress the concerns of francophones.

As Liberal activist Darryl Raymaker noted, however, "Many English-speaking people across Canada, Albertans prominent among them, were outraged at the federal government 'shoving French down our throats'" (Raymaker 2017, 151). With oilmen and farmers already skeptical about Trudeau, the passage of the Official Languages Act in July, 1969, increased the sense of Western resentment towards Trudeau and his government.

A few months later, prominent Calgary lawyer Milt Harradence began to openly question the West's place within Canada. As Raymaker described him, "Harradence was a high profile, revolver-packing, headline-seeking criminal lawyer (and former skilled RCAF pilot) who had grown up in Prince Alberta, Saskatchewan, where he'd fallen under the spell of its finest criminal lawyer, John Diefenbaker" (Raymaker 2017, 154).

Harradence had also been leader of the Alberta Progressive Conservative Party in the 1963 provincial election. He resigned as leader after the party won no seats, but remained involved politically. According to Raymaker, in "February 1970 Harradence announced the formation of the New West Task Force, comprising Calgary businessmen and ordinary citizens who wanted economic consultants to study the feasibility of an independent western Canada" (Raymaker 2017, 154).

Harradence received numerous calls offering support as well as requests to speak. Calgary radio talk show host Bill Knights reported that two-thirds of his callers were favourable towards Western secessionism. Additionally, Robert Thompson, the Progressive

Conservative MP for Red Deer and former leader of the federal Social Credit Party, said that the secessionist movement only needed a leader for it to pose a threat to Canadian unity.

However, as Raymaker wrote, "All this western alienation ballyhoo continued at a reduced noise level through the summer of 1970 and Harradence's task force never delivered a report" (Raymaker 2017, 159).

Indeed, the incipient secessionist movement was thwarted by the "October Crisis" of 1970, when a left-wing Quebec terrorist organization, the Front de libération du Québec (FLQ), kidnapped Quebec cabinet minister Pierre Laporte and British trade commissioner James Cross. To deal with this situation, Trudeau invoked the War Measures Act, thereby suspending habeas corpus, and giving extraordinary powers to police. The army was also out in force.

Trudeau's decisive action was very popular across the country, and notably in Alberta. A public opinion poll conducted the following month found that 80 percent of Canadians supported Trudeau's use of the War Measures Act while only 10 percent were opposed. And in an interview, Alberta's Social Credit Premier Harry Strom, "said that he completely supported the federal government's response to the Quebec crisis, and in his view so did 95 percent of Alberta's citizens" (Raymaker 2017, 166-167).

Trudeau's newfound support in Alberta was the death-knell of the embryonic secessionist movement. As Raymaker put it, gone "were the rabble-rousers of western alienation; Harradence's task force disappeared permanently. Alberta public opinion had rarely been more unconditionally Canadian than in those dark days of October 1970" (Raymaker 2017, 165).

However, support for secessionism was only temporarily dead and would rekindle within a few short years. The Independent Alberta Association (IAA) – the first serious separatist organization – would be formed in 1974.

Federal Oil Export Tax

The formation of the IAA in 1974 is very understandable in light of Pierre Trudeau's energy policies.

In September 1973, Trudeau's government imposed a Federal Oil Export Tax to siphon revenues out of Alberta. Premier Peter Lougheed stated that the tax "appears to be the most discriminatory action taken by a federal government against a particular province in the entire history of Confederation." Lougheed went on to note that, "The natural resources of the provinces are owned by the provinces under the terms of Confederation. The action taken by Ottawa strikes at the very roots of Confederation" (Wood 1985, 147).

A few months later Lougheed said, "We view the federal export tax on Alberta oil as contrary to both the spirit and intent of Confederation. It is discriminatory, and is a price freeze on all of Alberta's oil production at immense cost to Albertans" (Wood 1985, 150).

After Liberal finance minister John Turner delivered his budget in November 1974, Lougheed explained that:

> Mr. Turner very conveniently ignores an export tax of one and a half billion dollars a year from the depleting oil wells of Alberta, wells that may only last for ten years. That takes out of the heritage of Alberta between $800 and $1,000 a year for every man, woman and child in our province. In essence . . . I guess it's probably the biggest ripoff of any province that's ever occurred in Confederation's history (Wood 1985, 155).

That ripoff would be superseded by a subsequent Liberal policy, the National Energy Program (NEP) in 1980, but not before Trudeau ran an intentionally divisive election campaign.

The 1980 election

In the federal election of May 1979, Joe Clark's Progressive Conservatives won a minority government, despite receiving a lower percentage of the popular vote than Trudeau's Liberals. Clark's government subsequently presented a budget in December and was immediately defeated in a confidence vote, necessitating a new election.

Energy, of course, had been a major political issue since 1973, and Trudeau decided to intensify regional cleavages as a way to get back into power. This was explicit in Liberal campaign materials. As John Duffy wrote, "The divisive appeal to regional interests was overt, as in one ad that depicted a grinning Clark cozying up to Alberta's Premier Lougheed. The voice-over stated, 'Ontarians should pay attention to the budget that demonstrates how easily Joe Clark would give in to Premier Lougheed and Alberta on energy prices. . .'" (Duffy 2002, 295).

Duffy further explained that "This policy thrust was carefully calculated to play on the party's regional strengths – Quebec, the Atlantic provinces, urban Ontario – while virtually writing off the country west of the Ontario-Manitoba border" (Duffy 2002, 295). Indeed, "Folks in the energy-producing provinces would soon understand that the Liberals wanted money to flow from their provincial governments and the oil companies that employed them to both eastern consumers and the government they controlled in Ottawa" (Duffy 2002, 298).

Previously, the Liberals liked to campaign on "national unity" but their new campaign strategy directly contradicted it. "But the Grits didn't care. In 1980 they dropped their unity message and ran on a bald program of redistributing wealth from the West to the East. As Keith Davey subsequently put it, 'Screw the West. We'll take the rest.' The Liberals figured that any western outrage would be more than offset elsewhere, especially Ontario" (Duffy 2002, 298).

They were right. Trudeau won a majority government with no seats in BC, Alberta, or Saskatchewan, and only two in Manitoba. Albertans knew that they were in trouble, and the separatist movement began organizing in earnest (Wagner, 2009).

National Energy Program

Trouble arrived in the form of the National Energy Program (NEP) in October 1980. As Progressive Conservative MP David Kilgour wrote:

The Liberals' NEP contained both an announced and an undeclared set of objectives. The four public ones seemed the soul of reason: greater energy self-sufficiency, conservation, 'nation-building' and Canadianization. The unspoken goal was clearly continued Liberal party hegemony in Central Canada at the expense of Western Canadians generally and Albertans in particular (Kilgour 1988, 95).

The publicly stated reasons offered by Trudeau and his cronies were largely a smokescreen. As Kilgour notes,

The Liberal party, having learned to govern with virtually no representation from the West, wished to be seen as the defender of Central Canada regardless of economic consequences in Western Canada. Indeed Marc Lalonde in a candid moment later confessed: "The major factor behind the NEP wasn't Canadianization or getting more from the industry or even self-sufficiency. The determinant factor was the fiscal imbalance between the provinces and the federal government…. Our proposal was to increase Ottawa's share appreciably, so that the share of the producing provinces would decline significantly and the industry's share would decline somewhat" (Kilgour 1988, 97-98).

The results of the NEP were devastating for Alberta.

Thousands of jobs in Western Canada were lost, primarily in the drilling and service sectors of the energy industry. Proposed mega-projects such as the Alsands plant at Fort McMurray were cancelled. Numerous western businesses went into bankruptcy. Many careers and families were broken; home mortgages were foreclosed in large numbers (Kilgour 1988, 98).

The NEP "blatantly discriminated against the western provinces, maintained the domestic price of conventional oil and gas resources at about half the world price, and subsidized the consumption of imported oil" (Kilgour 1988, 98).

In short, Pierre Trudeau unleashed a kind of economic siege against Alberta from about 1973 until he left office over ten years later. This sort of attack on one particular region or province was unprecedented in Canadian history.

The centralizing purpose of the *Charter of Rights*

Besides the NEP, another major thrust of Trudeau's efforts was constitutional change. He was the primary initiator behind the development and adoption of the *Charter of Rights*.

Throughout his political life, Trudeau aggressively pushed Canada in a left-wing direction, and the *Charter* was a key component of that goal. There can be no doubt that it has been used as a judicial tool to dramatically reorient the country in an increasingly leftward direction.

Interestingly, one key purpose of the *Charter* was to reduce Canadians' attachments to their provinces and increase their affinity for the central government.

Since Confederation in 1867, Canada has been a federal state. In a large country such as Canada, federalism is beneficial because governments in each province can enact policies favoured by their own citizens. Therefore, the regional diversity of the country is reflected in a diversity of policies. This jurisdictional diversity also contributes to the development of different provincial identities. Canadians in various parts of the country often identify more closely with their provinces than with the national government.

Trudeau saw such regional diversity and identity as potential threats to national unity. However, he believed he could mitigate regionalist loyalties through a new national "Charter of Rights and Freedoms."

Trudeau's purpose of reducing regional diversity and loyalty through a national Charter is explained in a book by University of British Columbia political scientist Alan C. Cairns entitled, *Charter versus Federalism: The Dilemmas of Constitutional Reform*. The very title of the book conveys the basic idea - Charter versus federalism – because the Charter is about a uniform, nation-wide application of "rights," whereas federalism is about each province adopting its own approach on multiple issues, leading to policy diversity across the country. There is a tension between these two concepts.

Cairns explained Trudeau's goal as follows:

> The Charter was always more than an instrument to protect
> the rights of Canadians against their governments. The larger
> political purpose, which explains its tenacious sponsorship
> by the federal government, was to strengthen national unity
> by providing constitutional support to a new definition of
> Canadians as a rights-bearing citizenry regardless of location.
> These rights, enforceable against both orders of government,
> were intended to strengthen the Canadian component of civic
> identity by being uniformly available and by limiting the
> capacity of federalism to generate diverse treatment of citizens
> as demarcated by provincial boundaries (Cairns 1992, 49-50).

That is, the *Charter* placed new limits on federalism by giving judges
the power – in at least some instances – to strike down provincial
legislation that had previously been immune to judicial oversight.
This would restrict the provinces in an important way because,
as Cairns notes, "every time the Charter nullifies a provincial
executive or legislative action, it limits provincial variations in
policy and administrative behaviour by invoking Canadian values.
In a competition between a Charter-sustained Canadian value and a
provincial value, the latter will lose" (Cairns 1992, 76-77). Institutions
of the central government – the Supreme Court of Canada using the
Charter of Rights – could overrule provincial policies and preferences.

Not only would provincial governments encounter new constraints,
but citizens would be encouraged to view their provinces as
subordinate to the more important national rights-granting document.
The consequence of such an outcome is very important: "A modified
and strengthened country-wide identity would, relatively, weaken
provincial senses of community and identity" (Cairns 1992, 118).

That is to say, it was a deliberate purpose of the *Charter* to weaken
people's attachments to their provinces. The *Charter* was intended to
generate a new Canadian national identity that would replace regional
or provincial identities with a greater affinity for the nation as a whole.

There is no doubt that Pierre Trudeau determined to fundamentally
transform the country. As Cairns put it, "post-Charter Canada was

intended to be recognizably different from pre-Charter Canada"
(Cairns 1992, 62), and it is.

Polling data on support for secession

As mentioned above, indications of support for Western separatism
first became apparent during Pierre Trudeau's first term, and initial
attempts at secessionist organizing also began at about the same time.
Nevertheless, polling data indicate support for separation to be in
the single-digit range throughout the 1970s. Beginning with the NEP
in 1980, however, support increased and has consistently been in
the double-digit range since then. That is, Pierre Trudeau generated
a seemingly permanent increase in support for secessionism within
Alberta.

Early polls on secessionist sentiment were described by political
scientists David Elton and Roger Gibbins in 1979. As they noted,
a 1969 provincial poll found that only 5 per cent of "respondents
expressed interest in even discussing the merits of separation." Five
years later, a 1974 survey conducted in Calgary found less than 4 per
cent "expressed even the most cautious support for separatism." And in
a 1977 survey commissioned by the *Calgary Herald*, only 2.7 per cent
said yes to the question, "Would you like Alberta to separate?" (Elton
and Gibbins 1979, 94).

Clearly – at least as far as polling data suggests – support for
independence was very low before 1980. The only exception to this
was a 1971 poll which found that 12 percent of Albertans agreed
with the statement, "Western Canada should have its own separate
government, independent of everyone else" (Gilsdorf 1979, 171).

However, it's clear from survey data that the effect of Trudeau's
October 1980 NEP announcement was immediate. On November 1,
1980, the *Calgary Herald* reported on a poll indicating that 23 per
cent of Albertans were in favour of Western Canadian independence.
A subsequent study – undertaken in Edmonton from February to April
1981 – found that "about one in four respondents either supported
Alberta independence or were willing to give their provincial
government a mandate to negotiate it" (Bell 2007, 343).

Surprisingly, in a March 1981 poll conducted by the Canada West

Foundation, 49 per cent of Albertans agreed with the statement: "Western Canadians get so few benefits from being part of Canada that they might as well go it on their own" (Bell 2007, 344). That question did not measure outright commitment to independence as such, but it does indicate strong dissatisfaction with Confederation. Nevertheless, it is not inconsistent with some later polling.

Much like the poll from the Canada West Foundation, a "poll of 710 Westerners conducted by Environics Research in March 1992 found that 42 per cent of respondents agreed with the question: 'Western Canada gets so few benefits from Confederation the region might as well be on its own'" (Harrison 1995, 310). At that time, of course, Brian Mulroney was prime minister, and like Pierre Trudeau, he catered to Central Canada at the expense of the West. In fact, Mulroney's policies led to the rise of the Reform Party.

In 2005, a poll found 35.6 per cent of Westerners agreed with the statement: "Western Canadians should begin to explore the idea of forming their own country" (Bell 2007, 351).

More recently, on October 9, 2018, Ipsos released poll results indicating that 25 percent of Albertans agreed with the statement: "My province would be better off if it separated from Canada." When Ipsos had asked that same question in 2001, 19 percent of Albertans agreed (Ipsos 2018, 3).

On February 5, 2019, the Angus Reid Institute released poll results indicating that separatist sentiment was quite strong in Alberta: "More than half of Albertans (52%) say they believe the west would be better off if it left Canada" (Angus Reid Institute 2019, 8).

It seems clear that Prime Minister Justin Trudeau's policies are leading to increasing support for independence in Alberta. He is following in his father's footsteps. Support for secession may be higher now than at any previous time.

Although the questions asked by these surveys differ from one another, they nevertheless all indicate a common trend: before 1980, polls generally showed support for Alberta independence to be in single digits, usually low single digits. After 1980, polls show support in the double digits, often a quarter of the population or more.

This suggests that a fundamental change occurred in 1980 as a result of Pierre Trudeau. Before him, Albertans really weren't interested in thinking about independence, but he made it respectable and credible. Support for independence never seems to have returned to the low single digit range again.

Now, his son Justin is building on his work of pushing Alberta out of Canada. Whether or not that is his intention, it is the result of his policies.

Conclusion

Pierre Trudeau instigated the development of the Alberta separatist movement with his anti-Alberta policies and his efforts to remake Canada in his ideological image. This chapter has briefly examined those policies and the effect they had on support for secessionism.

Pierre's son, our current prime minister, has done much to revive and enhance the secessionist movement. This second Trudeau has made Alberta's plight even more severe, and therefore impossible to ignore. Justin Trudeau is the Alberta secessionist movement's biggest asset. The next chapter takes a brief look at the current crisis he's generated that is fueling support for creating a new country.

Chapter 3

THE CURRENT CRISIS

Alberta is currently facing a future of economic difficulties due to Justin Trudeau's climate change policies, which seem to receive strong support in Central Canada. Among these policies is Bill C-69, the *Impact Assessment Act*, which overhauled how major infrastructure projects in Canada are reviewed and approved. The National Energy Board was replaced with the Canadian Energy Regulator, and the approval process was made more difficult. Since project approvals will now be so difficult, critics called C-69 the "No More Pipelines Bill." It became law in 2019.

On top of that was Bill C-48, *The Oil Tanker Moratorium Act*, which prevents the export of crude oil from Alberta through ports on the coast of British Columbia. The purpose of this legislation is to help landlock Alberta's oil. It, too, became law in 2019.

Professor Ted Morton of the University of Calgary argues that as a result of Trudeau's policies, Alberta is losing control of its natural resources. As mentioned previously, section 92(A) of the constitution was added in 1982 as part of Pierre Trudeau's constitutional package to clarify provincial ownership and control of natural resources. But that constitutional protection is being effectively subverted by the federal government. As Morton writes,

> Alberta and the West now face the prospect of an important constitutional victory being reversed by another Liberal government led by yet another Prime Minister Trudeau. The cumulative effects of the Trudeau climate change policies, the recently enacted Bills C-69 and C-48, and the federally-

imposed carbon tax, will leave section 92(A) and the Alberta economy in tatters (Morton 2020, 25-26).

In fact, he writes, Trudeau's carbon tax "is a transparent attempt by the Liberal government to do indirectly what section 92A prohibits it from doing directly" (Morton 2020, 26).

The Supreme Court of Canada upheld the validity of Trudeau's carbon tax, the *Greenhouse Gas Pollution Pricing Act*, on March 25, 2021. In his dissent to the ruling, Supreme Court justice Russell Brown also saw the carbon tax as violating the Constitution. Brown called the *Greenhouse Gas Pollution Pricing Act* ruling "a model of federalism that rejects our Constitution and rewrites the rules of Confederation." He went on to state that "Its implications go far beyond the (carbon tax law), opening the door to federal intrusion — by way of the imposition of national standards — into all areas of provincial jurisdiction, including intra-provincial trade and commerce, health, and the management of natural resources." Furthermore, he wrote, "It is bound to lead to serious tensions in the federation" (Platt 2021b, A4).

In short, with this decision, the Supreme Court of Canada allowed the federal government to circumvent the constitutional guarantee of provincial control of natural resources. The implications for Alberta's future are clearly ominous.

The second NEP

Another University of Calgary political scientist, Tom Flanagan, also wrote about how Alberta's oil resources have been blockaded by the federal government in the name of preventing climate change. He calls these climate change policies a second NEP. It has both differences and similarities to the original NEP:

> This second National Energy Program is different from the first; it seeks not to transfer Alberta's wealth to other governments but to reduce Alberta's use of its hydrocarbon resources to generate wealth, even if it also reduces incomes and wealth in other provinces. But it is similar in that it was calculated to appeal to voters in Ontario and Quebec for whom climate change was a priority issue. And it worked. It's not a coincidence that in 2015 Justin Trudeau was the first Liberal

leader to win a majority of seats from Quebec since his father did in 1980 (Flanagan 2020, 50).

Flanagan also summarized how environmentalists are working to stop the production of Alberta's oil:

> The long-term strategy of the climate alarmists is to cap the size of Alberta's oil industry by preventing the construction of new pipelines, then gradually euthanize the industry as alternative sources of energy become available. The link with the past is that, despite constitutional guarantees, federal politicians as well as those in other provinces still see western resources as subservient to "the purposes of the Dominion." They feel free to dispose of these resources in ways that they would never attempt for a natural resource such as hydroelectricity in Quebec (Flanagan 2020, 50).

In looking at solutions to Alberta's predicament, Flanagan offered a warning to those who think constitutional changes will be sufficient to solve the current problems:

> Constitutional change appears to offer certainty because the provisions of the constitution are beyond the reach of ordinary legislation or judicial decision. But the lesson of Canadian history, as far as Western resources are concerned, is that political pressure can always find a way to get around the constitution. Courts can explain rights away, and Parliament can circumvent ownership rights if it cannot go straight through them. Thus, 150 years after Louis Riel started the struggle for Western provinces to control their own public lands and natural resources, Alberta finds its resources blockaded. The great constitutional victories of 1930 and 1982 each lasted for a generation or two until outside forces succeeded in frustrating them (Flanagan 2020, 54-55).

If Flanagan is right – and he is – the constitutional changes many Westerners desire would not provide the security they are seeking. A federal government under the control of Central Canada will always have tools at its disposal to circumvent constitutional protections to achieve its goals at the expense of the West. Only independence can truly solve this problem.

Fiscal transfers

Whenever Albertans complain about how unfair Canada is to the
West, the issue of equalization payments is mentioned. Equalization
payments, however, are only one component of the fiscal transfers
Alberta makes to the federal government, and from there to other
provinces. Government programs such as Employment Insurance and
the Canada Pension Plan also result in money being transferred from
Alberta to other provinces. That is not the intentional design of these
policies as such, but it occurs due to Alberta's strong economy and
relatively younger population.

For decades, the expert on this topic has been University of Calgary
economist Robert Mansell. Recently he calculated the financial
transfers to and from each province during the period 1961-2018. To
make comparisons more understandable, he provided the figures in per
capita amounts:

> Taking all federal tax, expenditure and transfer policies into
> account, there were only five years (1961-1965) when Alberta
> was a net beneficiary. During this period the average annual net
> fiscal benefit to the province amounted to $483 per person. In
> every other year since then Alberta has been a net contributor.
> Indeed, it was by far the largest net fiscal contributor over the
> period 1974-1985, with an average annual net contribution
> of $7512 per person, and over the period 1993-2018, with an
> average annual net contribution of $4546 per person. The large
> net transfers from Alberta in the earlier period were primarily
> related to the interregional transfers associated with federal
> energy policies. These substantial transfers from Alberta
> would appear to constitute the largest interregional transfer in
> Canadian history (Mansell 2020, 112).

Put another way, "In terms of total dollars, Alberta has been a net fiscal
contributor in every year since 1965, amounting to a net contribution
of $630 billion" (Mansell 2020, 125).

That's a lot of money gone, and the consequence has been a significant
negative impact on Alberta. Mansell explained that these sorts of
transfers affect provincial incomes, employment and population.
According to his calculations, "the redistribution away from Alberta

in the most recent decade has worked to lower employment and population by over 12 per cent and reduce real incomes by more than 8 per cent" (Mansell 2020, 125). Unsurprisingly, transferring billions of dollars out of Alberta has harmed the province's economy and lowered its standard of living.

The message to Alberta

There are those from other parts of Canada who have recognized the injustices being done to Alberta. Perhaps the best example is *National Post* columnist Rex Murphy. On many occasions he has explained how the policies of Justin Trudeau's government have been harmful to Alberta.

Murphy clearly understands the implications of Trudeau's embrace of the Paris Agreement on climate change. In his view, there is a stark choice to be made: The Government of Canada must choose between energy development or the obligations imposed by the Agreement. Either the oil industry centred in Calgary will prosper, or the commitments made in Paris will be met. It will be one or the other.

Murphy portrayed this conflict in a way that makes a clear impression. As the title of one column puts it, "PM must choose: Paris or Calgary?" As he explained, "The real equation is not climate change AND the economy. It is climate change OR the economy. You have to choose. Paris or Calgary" (Murphy 2020a, A8).

He's right, that is the crucial choice. A prime minister representing all of Canada would choose the city in his own country. But a prime minister who governs for the benefit of the two central provinces can choose the foreign city, and the international accolades that go along with it. After all, Trudeau is probably more popular in Paris than in Calgary.

Late in 2020, Murphy criticized Trudeau's newly announced $170-per-tonne carbon tax. Again, his main concern was the effect it will have on Alberta, not only the jobs lost, but the message that it sends:

> The financial and employment repercussions are obvious.
> But the accumulation of these assaults has signalled to most
> Albertans that their province, and their concerns, are purely

secondary and tangential; that they are the lamb to be offered to the more noble global commitments and aspirations of their own federal government (Murphy 2020b, A12).

More recently, Alberta has experienced the cancellation of the Keystone XL pipeline by President Joe Biden. This event should have elicited much condemnation from Justin Trudeau's government, due to the damage that will result to Canada's economy, and especially to Alberta. Instead, Trudeau didn't even express the slightest concern. In a powerful column entitled, "Were I an Albertan, I'd be asking: What's the point?" Murphy described Trudeau's attitude towards the cancellation: "And after all, it's only Alberta. It's not like it's an attack on our auto industry, or, good heavens, Bombardier, which of course pose no 'threat' to our planet, and besides have the good grace to be positioned in real provinces, like Ontario and Quebec" (Murphy 2021, A14).

With genuine concern, Murphy explained the implications of the decision:

> And out in Alberta, it is becoming more and more difficult, perhaps even impossible, to answer the basic question: If you allow the savaging of our economy, if you ignore what we in Alberta have contributed to you during the good times, if you side with rabid environmentalism, pour on carbon taxes and fuel emission standards, if you bar every effort to build even one damn pipeline: Why are we in this thing? That's the question. And you know what "this thing" refers to (Murphy 2021, A14).

Clearly, Murphy understands that Liberal policies are pushing Alberta out of the country. Justin Trudeau's government is providing the impetus for the current rise of Alberta separatism.

Conclusion

The kinds of economic factors discussed in this chapter are what usually occupy people's minds when discussions about Alberta's future within Canada take place. Those who support secession from Canada invariably talk about the wealth that an independent Alberta would have at its disposal because that wealth would no longer be transferred elsewhere. Clearly, everyone in Alberta would benefit, if only through well-financed government programs such as health care and a new pension program.

However, there must be more to a country than economic considerations. Ties to the political community must transcend money. Money is important, of course, but loyalties must go deeper. Soldiers don't risk their lives defending their country because they are earning money, but because they believe something more important than money is at stake. They believe in the importance of their community.

Alberta's historic and cultural distinctiveness provides the basis for a unique provincial identity. This identity can help tie together the citizens of a newly independent Alberta. Exploring this topic is the purpose of the next chapter.

Chapter 4

Alberta's History and Identity

The desire of many Albertans to secede from Canada is usually driven by economic considerations. Policies of the federal government that redistribute large amounts of wealth from Alberta to other provinces, particularly Quebec, create a lot of anger. This is especially galling when the federal government and its Central Canadian support base are simultaneously thwarting the development of Alberta's energy resources, the very activity that generates Alberta's wealth in the first place.

Economic considerations will likely always be the main driver of secessionist sentiment. This contrasts sharply with the Quebec situation, where language and culture are the main issues motivating the drive for independence.

However, Alberta has some cultural differences from the rest of the country as well. This is important because Alberta secessionism needs to be based on more than simple economic calculations. The financial concerns are true and just, but there is more to a country than monetary considerations. Ties to a country must include a concept of identity. As this chapter will explain, there is an Alberta identity that is valuable and worthy of patriotic love.

Are Westerners really Canadians?

What is a Canadian? One answer would be, any person with Canadian citizenship. That is probably a sufficient answer for most people.

On that basis, basically every Western Canadian qualifies as a real Canadian.

But what if the question - "What is a Canadian?" - was asked, instead, about the country's national identity? Do Westerners qualify as Canadians under the criteria of Canadian national identity? The answer to this question is more problematic.

A nation's identity refers to the way in which its citizens see themselves as being distinct from citizens of other countries. In his book about America's national identity entitled *Who Are We?*, the late Harvard political scientist Samuel P. Huntington wrote, "Identity is an individual's or a group's sense of self. It is a product of self-consciousness, that I or we possess distinct qualities as an entity that differentiates me from you and us from them" (Huntington 2005, 21). He adds that, "Identities are imagined selves: they are what we think we are and what we want to be" (Huntington 2005, 22). Identity, in other words, is how we think of ourselves in relation to others.

It should not just be assumed that since Westerners live in a geographical part of Canada that they automatically embrace Canada's national identity. Instead, this matter requires careful analysis. The person who has done the most thinking on this question is political scientist Barry Cooper of the University of Calgary. As it turns out, he believes that the political identity of Westerners is different from that of Eastern Canadians. In his view, what is commonly referred to as "Canadian identity" is actually a concept that is primarily derived from – and relevant for - southern Ontario.

To understand the question of national identity, it is essential to look at Canadian history. The first major wave of English-speaking settlement into Canada consisted of colonists who had supported the British authorities in the American War of Independence. These colonials wanted to continue to live under British rule and therefore migrated to southern Ontario (formerly Upper Canada) and the Maritimes. They were known as "Loyalists."

A generation later, these same people and their children had to defend themselves against American incursions during the War of 1812. Because of their conflicts with and hostility towards the United States, the Loyalists of southern Ontario developed what Cooper calls a "garrison mentality" whereby they saw themselves as a beleaguered community, constantly on guard. This concept of the garrison became their "imaginative reality," or how they understood their community in relation to the rest of the world.

The experience of these early residents of Ontario, first as refugees from hostile Americans, then as defenders of their land against American invasion, explains the origin and prevalence of anti-American sentiment in Canada.

Due to the demographic and political pre-eminence of southern Ontario within Canada, its own identity became the basis for Canadian national identity. As Cooper writes, "Canada, the imaginative reality centred in the Loyalist heartland, became Canada the political reality." In other words, "there is indeed a Canadian identity, but it is restricted to the Loyalist heartland" (Cooper 1984, 216).

However, the garrison mentality of southern Ontario did not take hold in the West. The people of the Western provinces had different historical experiences than those of southern Ontario and therefore developed a different imaginative reality: "Western regional identity, to the extent that it is distinct from 'Canadian' identity, refers to distinct experiences expressed by way of distinct symbols and themes" (Cooper 1984, 218-219).

The stories of the West are different from those of Ontario, and that is important according to Cooper: "Stories, including the systematic stories we call history, reveal meanings, local and particular ones first of all, and through them general and universal ones. History, too, is a source of identity; historical literature also shows who we are and where is here because it recounts what was done and said" (Cooper 1984, 222).

Consequently, since the West does not see itself as a transplanted Ontario garrison, it is not imaginatively part of Canada. That is, because the historical experiences of Westerners were so different from those of southern Ontario, Westerners don't share with Ontarians the same understanding of what it means to be Canadian.

This has implications for the idea of national unity. As Cooper puts it, "national unity is a symbol expressing 'Canadian' identity, the identity of the Loyalist heartland" (Cooper 1984, 218). That is to say, it's not truly "national" at all. Instead, it largely involves advancing the regional interest of a certain part of Canada (i.e., Ontario) under the guise of what's best for all of Canada.

Many Westerners have a strong regional identity and therefore feel a closer bond with the West than with Canada as a whole. This is fundamental to Western imaginative reality. Cooper explains as follows:

> Regional identity is at the heart of Western political consciousness. For many Westerners, as for many francophone Quebecers, the significant public realm is not Canada but the region or province. Canada for them is, first and perhaps last, a legal structure that performs certain administrative functions. It is not first of all a collective political reality, nor an important source of meaning or pride, save under exceptional circumstances. In contrast, the region, the West, carries a constant and positive emotional valence: it is here and us (Cooper 1984, 213).

Of course, not all Westerners identify more closely with the West than with Canada as a whole but many of us do. For us, Cooper's analysis explains something that we have sensed but were previously unable to clearly understand and articulate. That is, the idea of Canadian identity presented to us expresses a different understanding of the country than the one we actually experience ourselves.

Westerners have long felt left out of important political and economic decisions in Canada. Historically, many federal policies were enacted at the expense of the West, with the NEP being the quintessential example. But according to Cooper's analysis, Westerners have also been left out of the common meaning of Canadian identity.

Alberta identity and Justin Trudeau's "postnational state"

More recently, even the concept of Canadian identity itself has been challenged by Prime Minister Justin Trudeau. Shortly after his election as prime minister in 2015, Trudeau told the *New York Times*, "There is no core identity, no mainstream in Canada," and that Canada is "the first postnational state."

The *Times* rightly explained that Justin's view makes him "an avatar of his father's vision." The social engineering of Justin's father, Prime Minister Pierre Trudeau, has been so successful that the historical notion of what it means to be Canadian has been increasingly eviscerated since the 1970s. Together, the Trudeaus have brought the idea of Canadian identity to its knees.

Central Canada may no longer have a "core identity" as Trudeau states, but Alberta has an identity.

As mentioned previously, Barry Cooper has argued that a community's stories form an important part of its identity, and history constitutes a key element of those stories. The West has its own stories and history, distinct from those of Eastern Canada, and this contributes to the West's unique regional identity.

Besides Cooper, Alberta has another prominent conservative thinker who has reflected on Western identity – Ted Byfield. Byfield, best known as the founder of *Alberta Report* and its sister publications, also initiated the creation of a 12-volume history set called "Alberta in the 20th Century." This project was surprisingly successful and the proceeds helped to keep the *Report* magazines afloat for a time.

However, the success of this popular history series was counterintuitive. Alberta is a small market, and the volumes were rather expensive. Why did they sell so well?

Byfield attributed the success, in part, to the emergence of an Alberta identity. In a January 1999 *Alberta Report* column he wrote,

> There is gradually developing in Alberta a very powerful provincial identity. Perhaps it's because we have so often been called "redneck" by the rest of Canada, perhaps because we have so often resisted trends in the rest of Canada, perhaps because we live closer to our frontier origins, perhaps because from our very beginning almost everything we produce must be sold on a world market, not a protected local one. And, finally, perhaps because our national identity has become so confused of late that it's hard to define what being a Canadian is supposed to mean. There's little doubt what being an Albertan means, and this has a deepening significance. That, we believe, is one of the chief reasons for the success of the history series (Byfield 1999, 2).

Here, years before Justin Trudeau declared that the country had "no core identity," Byfield had already recognized that "it's hard to define what being a Canadian is supposed to mean." At the same time, however, there's "little doubt what being an Albertan means," and his Alberta history series was deliberately intended to strengthen that identity as well.

In his Foreword to the first volume of the series, *The Great West Before 1900*, Byfield explained his purpose for producing these books. He began by recounting a discussion he had with a young man from Texas. Byfield asked the fellow why Texas was known as the Lone Star State. The fellow replied that Texas had been a republic for about ten years and then had a war with Mexico, which is when the famous battle for the Alamo occurred. Most interestingly, the Texan had said that's when "we" had a war with Mexico and then "we" joined the United States. As Byfield explained, "Utterly unconscious of what he was doing, this young man identified himself with events that occurred nearly a century and a half before he was born. It wasn't what 'they' did, it was what 'we' did. Whatever happened to Texas then, he was somehow involved in it" (Byfield 1991b, x).

Albertans and other Canadians don't often talk that way and Byfield believes that's because we "do not identify with our own past." For us, what happened in the past is what "they" did not what "we" did. Some people see this as a good thing because, in their view, we should have a cool and dispassionate approach to the past rather than an enthusiastic commitment to our province (or country) and its accomplishments. Those people are concerned about "the dangers of jingoism and blind tribal loyalty." As Byfield explained, however, that perspective has led to a form of rootlessness and lack of belonging which is basically the opposite of the mentality of the young Texan noted above.

Byfield wanted his history books to correct the erroneous perspective that effectively divorces us from our own history. As he wrote, "Candidly, we want the Albertans who read them to come away from them saying 'we' not 'they'" (Byfield 1991b, x).

Byfield believes Alberta's history is worth learning. And as we study it, "we may find we come away with a certain assurance, a strange sense of common purpose, a feeling of continuity with our past. No longer are we homeless. We know now where we live. We belong" (Byfield 1991b, xi). This is precisely what Cooper meant when he wrote of the importance of history to a community's identity – it shows us who "we" are.

Justin Trudeau says that Canada no longer has a "core identity." Well, as Ted Byfield so clearly pointed out, Alberta still has an identity, one that needn't be lost to leftist dreamers in Ottawa. For those who would like to learn more about it, there's no better place to start than his "Alberta in the 20th Century" history books.

Alberta's history and its spirit of defiance

In a subsequent volume in that series, Byfield also explained the value of knowing Alberta's history. After describing the attitude of purpose and resolve that drove the pioneers to overcome seemingly insurmountable difficulties, he noted that the early pioneer fervor would eventually dissipate. He then added, "Yet times of great human accomplishment endure, for they have two functions for a society. First they serve as a trigger, they start things going. And just as important, they serve as a model. They lay down the foundation, set the tone, establish an identity. So much of history, say the sceptics, is mere folklore. What do they mean, 'mere?'" (Byfield 1992, vii).

At this point he described particular experiences faced by some pioneers: an immigrant farmer from eastern Europe kissing the ground when he finally arrives at his Alberta homestead; a mother using needle and thread to sew up her child's severe injury; a Mountie trudging through snow on a cold winter day to check on the safety of a remote farm family; a doctor racing a buggy across the prairie to attend to a woman in labour. He then adds, "And when all these and hundreds of other such stories are put together into one comprehensive whole, they are showing us what it means to be an Albertan" (Byfield 1992, vii).

These stories, and others of their kind, help us to understand what Alberta is as a community. Byfield continued, "So it's all folklore. Let's hope so, and let's pray that this volume contributes to it in some small way. For without folklore, without a common tradition upon which we all stand, neither this province nor this country has any chance whatever of living through another century" (Byfield 1992, vii).

It is this "folklore" (stories passed down from one generation to another) that tells us who we are as a community and it is therefore a vital element in preserving the community into the future. History provides the common story that ties us together as Albertans.

One of the pivotal stories of Alberta's history – the election of a Social Credit government – set the province apart from much of the rest of the country. As Byfield noted in his Foreword to Volume 6 of the history series, *Fury and Futility: The Onset of the Great Depression 1930-1935*, Alberta was brought to the attention of the world by the election of William "Bible Bill" Aberhart's Social Credit Party on August 22, 1935. Byfield explained that,

> On that day, Alberta launched out onto its own. Whether it was for good or for ill, people still argue about. In fact, nothing has ever divided us so fiercely. Our internecine struggle appalled and fascinated reporters from all over the country. We became distinct, unique, "crazy" according to a headline in the *Boston Globe*. Yet it also defined us. Alberta's reaction to the Depression was different. We would not capitulate and let it hammer us. We would fight back. That is our reputation (Byfield 1998a, vii).

Byfield reiterated this point in his Foreword to Volume 7, *Aberhart and the Alberta Insurrection 1935-1940*, where he wrote, "While other provinces whined about the Depression, Alberta acted. We would not acquiesce in the misery we felt and saw around us. We would fight. We would rebel. If anything is characteristic of this province, it's that spirit of defiance. Push us far enough and we will strike back. That was our record and that is our reputation" (Byfield 1998b, vi).

Clearly, the election of a Social Credit government that would last for 36 years is not just an historical anecdote. It had a formative effect upon the province and its political culture. Furthermore, it created an image of Alberta distinctiveness that remains to this day. As Byfield put it, "Alberta's venture into Social Credit in the final five years of the calamitous Thirties left a lasting legacy. In the political lore of the rest of Canada, particularly in Ontario, it established Alberta as a radical province, the home of an unstable electorate prone to perilous political experimentation" (Byfield 1998b, vi).

The study of Alberta's history reveals how this province got its reputation for being different from the rest of the country. The election of Social Credit in 1935 indicated that Alberta had a "spirit of defiance," as Byfield put it. Byfield himself and his *Alberta Report* also clearly embodied Alberta's spirit of defiance, frequently tangling with elements of Canada's mainstream media and defending Alberta's position in national debates.

Alberta's conservative political culture

One widespread conception of Alberta is that it has a more conservative political culture than the rest of Canada. Such a view can be supported by looking at the province's voting record since the 1930s; at both the federal and provincial levels, Albertans have voted overwhelmingly for right-leaning parties. The accidental NDP government (2015-2019) was elected with less than 41 percent of the vote because right-of-centre voters – totaling 52 percent – were divided between the Wildrose and Progressive Conservative parties.

Besides Alberta's voting record, there are also other evidences of a conservative political culture. Jared Wesley, a political scientist at the University of Alberta, has provided historical confirmation of the conventional view of Alberta as a conservative-oriented province.

Wesley examines what he calls "political codes." Generally speaking, political "codes" can be understood as the expressions of a broadly accepted belief system, or a set of prevailing political values that dominate the thinking of political leaders in a community. They can also be seen as patterns of political thought and behaviour. To quote Wesley's definition, written in academic jargon, "a code is a unique discursive paradigm that persists among dominant elites in a given community over time" (Wesley 2011, 11).

When Wesley compared the political cultures of Alberta, Saskatchewan, and Manitoba, he found that each of these provinces has a unique "political code." After an analysis of the historical trajectories of the three provinces, he reduces the political code of each province down to one word. For Alberta, that word is "freedom," for Saskatchewan it's "security," and for Manitoba it's "moderation."

How can a community's political code be determined? There may be various ways of doing so, but Wesley chose to examine the election campaign literature and political platforms of Alberta's principal provincial parties since the 1930s, that is, the Social Credit and Progressive Conservative parties. As he noted, "political cultures are actively promoted, transmuted, and transmitted by dominant political parties" (Wesley 2011, 3).

In his analysis, Wesley identified three core elements of Alberta's freedom-based political code. The first component is populism, which emphasizes freedom from government overreach, whether that government be in Edmonton or Ottawa.

The second core element of Alberta's political code is individualism. Wesley writes,

> Throughout much of the past seven decades, Social Credit and Conservative Party rhetoric has stressed the primacy of the individual as the core unit of society. In their platforms, we find constant reference to individual initiative, free enterprise, hard work, and a general go-it-alone philosophy - all of which correspond to the conservatism embedded in the province's political culture (Wesley 2011, 12).

The third core element of Alberta's political code is the feeling of alienation from the centre of decision-making in Eastern Canada. As a result of this, both the Social Credit and Progressive Conservative parties have promoted the autonomy of the provincial state at certain points during their tenures in power.

To summarize, then, Wesley writes that, "Together, these three pillars - populism, individualism, and provincial autonomy - have helped structure Alberta politics around a freedom-based narrative that, itself, draws on the major aspects of the province's political culture" (Wesley 2011, 12).

Besides describing Alberta's political code, Wesley provides an explanation for how it developed historically. Interestingly, he focuses on early American immigration into Alberta as the most important factor. That is, the large number of American settlers arriving in Alberta during the early twentieth century brought with them three key political values, each of which became a core element of Alberta's political code.

Wesley writes that the first key value was "a laissez-faire brand of frontier liberalism that, over time, has become the foundation of Albertan conservatism." The second was "a penchant for radicalism - a distinct lack of deference - that has manifested itself in a persistent populist impulse." And the third was "a synthetic form of anticolonialism vis-à-vis central Canada, through which a strong sense of western alienation has been expressed for several generations" (Wesley 2011, 55).

In short, American homesteaders can be credited (or blamed) for setting Alberta on the pathway of political conservatism from its early days.

Once the path was set, however, Alberta's major political parties have continued to carry and transmit the same basic values through their efforts. Wesley put it this way:

> Alberta's two most successful parties have spoken to the public with a common accent. Emphasizing three core elements of freedom - individualism, populism, and provincial autonomy - Social Credit and the Progressive Conservatives have cultivated a dominant narrative that has helped sustain their province's conservative political culture. Indeed, their campaign appeals have often involved explicit references to

American values, sources, and texts imported by the province's founding fragment (Wesley 2011, 111).

The major point of all this, of course, is to provide historical evidence for the popular view that Alberta is more politically conservative than the other provinces. The stereotype is based on fact. It's not a mistake or misconception. As Wesley suggests, "Measured by their popularity at the polls, the Socreds' and Tories' common vision of Alberta as a conservative society has dominated political discourse as much as the parties have dominated the legislature" (Wesley 2011, 113). In short, Alberta has a distinct conservative political culture.

Christianity and political conservatism in Alberta's history

Another University of Alberta political scientist, Clark Banack, offers a somewhat different explanation of Alberta's conservative political culture. He argues that it is the result of the influence of evangelical Christianity on a number of Alberta's political leaders. His analysis involves detailed examinations of certain political leaders' religious views.

The United Farmers of Alberta (UFA) was founded as a lobby group for farmers in 1909, but later decided to run candidates for election. It won the provincial election of 1921 and remained in power until 1935. The most influential figure in the UFA was Henry Wise Wood, its president from 1916 to 1931. Although most other farm leaders were influenced by socialism to one degree or another, Wood was not, and he believed that an ideal society could only be realized by the voluntary co-operation of godly citizens.

Wood's efforts to discourage support for socialism among Alberta's farmers had a long-term impact on Alberta's politics. Banack writes,

> Wood rejected both the secular intellectual solutions of Marx and the Christian-based social gospel calls for socialism and placed the onus squarely on the individual to bring about the perfect democratic and economic system. In doing so,

> Wood helped to steer early Alberta society in a decidedly anti-socialistic and more individualistic direction by harnessing the Prairie-wide utopian and co-operative hopes of Alberta agrarians to a stern emphasis on individual responsibility (Banack 2016, 95-96).

Thus, the origin of Alberta's generally anti-socialistic perspective goes back at least 100 years to the leadership of Henry Wise Wood and his Christian individualism.

Shortly after Wood left the presidency of the UFA, William "Bible Bill" Aberhart of Calgary started the Alberta Social Credit Party. Aberhart was a public school principal who was best known as a popular Christian radio broadcaster with a huge listening audience in the province. When the Great Depression hit Alberta causing widespread hardship and despair, Aberhart began to use his radio program to promote Social Credit economics as the solution.

When the Alberta Social Credit Party won the 1935 provincial election (ousting the UFA which had abandoned Wood's anti-socialism), Aberhart became premier. He remained premier until he died in 1943. Throughout his term as premier he continued preaching the gospel on his radio broadcast.

After Aberhart's death his chief lieutenant, Ernest Manning, became Alberta's premier and head of Aberhart's radio ministry. It's important to note that Manning, like Aberhart before him, continued the work of radio evangelism even as premier. This is because both Aberhart and Manning believed "that economic oppression was rooted in the depravity of man and that society's only hope to fully rectify the situation was wide-scale religious conversion, or rebirth, at an individual level" (Banack 2016, 150). In other words, political problems could only be solved as citizens turned to Christ for salvation. In this respect, there was a relationship between the radio evangelism and political activities of these two premiers.

Like Henry Wise Wood before him, Ernest Manning was strongly opposed to socialism. Banack writes that "Manning's approach to governance while premier was characterized by a stern and unflinching defence of a free-market economy" (Banack 2016, 137).

In short, "working from a distinctly religious position that guided their thinking about politics, Aberhart and especially Manning did much to guide Alberta on an anti-collectivist trajectory that is largely unique among Canadian provinces" (Banack 2016, 154).

Ted Byfield and *Alberta Report*

Although not a political leader as such, one of the most influential Alberta opinion leaders during the latter part of the twentieth century was the aforementioned Ted Byfield. He was the founder of *Alberta Report* magazine which was published from 1973 to 2003 (sometimes under slightly different names). That magazine had a distinct conservative and generally Christian perspective. Because of its popularity and large circulation, it had a substantial impact on Alberta society and politics.

It's hard to overstate the significant role *Alberta Report* filled during its existence. Referring to the days before the World Wide Web, Ted Morton, the University of Calgary political scientist and former provincial finance minister, is quoted by Banack as saying, "Alberta Report was our Internet, it was our website, Facebook and Twitter . . . in those early years [of conservative activism], almost all roads passed through Alberta Report" (Banack 2016, 161).

Alberta Report vigorously defended conservative views on a whole range of contemporary issues. According to Banack, the

> essence of Byfield's social thought—the message that most easily resonated with readers—was the notion that the vast majority of the ills of contemporary society, including crime, domestic abuse, family breakup, and even rampant government spending leading to chronic deficits, could be traced back

to the declining influence of traditional Christian values, especially as they pertained to the norms governing sexual behaviour (Banack 2016, 161).

The magazine had an important role to fill in the culture war. "Responding to 'the systematic attempt to abolish religious influence on the law and society,' Byfield utilized *Alberta Report* as a vital tool within the larger battle to gradually re-establish traditional Christian morality in the minds of citizens" (Banack 2016, 162).

Importantly, Ted Byfield, like Aberhart and Manning in previous years, recognized that social change could only be realized if citizens would turn to Christ: "'To change society, you must preach the gospel,' noted Byfield" (Banack 2016, 163).

Preston Manning and the Reform Party of Canada

Ted Byfield played a key role in the creation of the Reform Party of Canada in 1987. However, Preston Manning (the son of former Premier Ernest Manning) was the first and only leader of the party. Like his father, Preston was an evangelical Christian and his religious views affected his political views.

In a 1987 speech describing the perspective of the new party, Preston noted that "while we uphold freedom of conscience for all citizens, we also acknowledge Canada's Judeo-Christian heritage and its value as a source of moral and ethical guidance" (Banack 2016, 188).

Like the previously discussed leaders, Manning knew that bigger government was not the answer to society's problems.

In summarizing the effect of evangelical Christianity on Alberta's overall political history, Banack writes, "it is quite significant to note that a certain religious interpretation has undergirded this populist, pro-market sentiment from Wood, through the thought of Aberhart and Ernest Manning, and into the thinking of Preston Manning in contemporary Alberta" (Banack 2016, 209).

American immigration and Alberta's cultural distinctiveness

Earlier, it was mentioned that Jared Wesley attributed Alberta's conservative political culture to the influence of American settlers. There's likely something to that. The people who originally settled Alberta had a formative influence on its culture. With this in mind, it is significant that Alberta welcomed a particularly large number of American immigrants, much more so than other provinces.

Nelson Wiseman, a political scientist at the University of Toronto, has written a lot about the political effect of American immigration on Alberta. According to him, the effect was substantial. As he writes, "In 1911, American-born Albertans (22 percent of the population) outnumbered the British-born, Ontario-born, and European-born. Almost certainly, this was the largest concentration of Americans in any jurisdiction outside the US" (Wiseman 2007, 244).

He adds that, "Americans and their ideas helped shape provincial politics because they settled in the politically determinative rural areas. Their influence was particularly pronounced in the south" (Wiseman 2007, 244).

Later, after the discovery of oil in 1947, more Americans came north to help in the development of the province's petroleum industry. According to Wiseman, "Between 1955 and 1970, nine of the fifteen presidents of Calgary's exclusive and influential Petroleum Club were Americans. In no other province were Americans so prominent as captains of industry" (Wiseman 2007, 247).

Besides the over-sized influence on the oil industry, something similar occurred in the realm of religion. Wiseman writes that, "Alberta has been the province most receptive to Christian evangelicalism. As early as 1908, the *Calgary Daily Herald* reported that American and central Canadian 'evangelists seem to have a grip on the city'" (Wiseman 2007, 255).

To a certain degree, this religious influence has carried over into politics because "Alberta resembles the US" in that "evangelical Christians have played leading political roles there" (Wiseman 2007, 255).

Wiseman points out that the connection between religion and politics is not just a phenomenon of the distant past, either: "That conservative religious influence lingers in Alberta can be seen in the federal party leaders recently produced by the province: Preston Manning, Stockwell Day, and Stephen Harper are all evangelical Christians" (Wiseman 2007, 256-257).

Wiseman is not alone in emphasizing the crucial role of immigration patterns on the province. In 1990, historians Howard and Tamara Palmer published a one-volume history of Alberta entitled *Alberta: A New History*. Among other things, the Palmers wanted to explain Alberta's conservative political culture, and like Wiseman, they root their explanation in immigration. However, their analysis differs somewhat from his because they suggest that, besides the Americans, certain Europeans also contributed to the right-leaning orientation of Alberta's political environment.

As a general point, the Palmers argue that the post-World War Two wave of immigration that flowed into the province, "contributed to the rightward shift in Alberta's political culture." In particular, they write that the political perspectives of eastern European immigrants escaping communism, "were among the many factors that helped to shift Alberta's political culture to the right during the 1950s and 1960s" (Palmer and Palmer 1990, 305).

But movement in the conservative direction didn't come just from eastern Europeans. Besides that group, there were also, "British immigrants fleeing socialism, conservative rural Dutch Calvinist immigrants, and the small-business oriented Germans, Austrians, and Scandinavians, who were usually leery of government regulation" (Palmer and Palmer 1990, 306).

Like Wiseman, however, the Palmers also note the disproportionate influence of Americans in the post-war period. Although their numbers were not large, a considerable number were prominent oilmen and, "Like their counterparts in the United States, they often held strong right-wing views" (Palmer and Palmer 1990, 306).

It should not be surprising that the culture of early settlers – and even the arrival of later immigrants – can have a profound impact on the culture of any society. The fact that Quebec was originally settled by people from France affects Canadian culture and politics every day.

Although Alberta was not founded by Americans in the way that Quebec was settled by the French, Americans constituted a disproportionate number of early settlers – and later pioneers of the oil industry. Their cultural and political influence helped to make Alberta different from the other provinces to some degree. In other words, the large numbers of American immigrants in the province's early decades, as well as during the post-war oil rush, helps to explain why Alberta is a culturally distinct region within Canada.

Albertan identity and anti-Albertanism in the East

According to Richard Avramenko, a political scientist at the University of Wisconsin-Madison, the American influence may contribute to the anti-Alberta attitudes of people in Central Canada. He explains this idea by looking at Canadian history. His analysis parallels that of Barry Cooper which was examined earlier, but it differs on certain key points.

To a large degree, English-speaking Canada began with the arrival of the Loyalists in the late 1700s. The Loyalists were the colonials who rejected the newly independent United States of America. They were so opposed to the creation of the new country that they came to Britain's northern colonies to remain under British rule. In today's terminology, the Loyalists were "anti-American."

This anti-Americanism was soon reinforced by the War of 1812. The Loyalists and their descendants literally had to fight off American invaders. As a result, they developed what would later be called a "garrison mentality," whereby they saw themselves as living within the defensive perimeter of Upper Canada (now known as Ontario).

These Loyalists were largely Protestant and frequently anti-Catholic. They were at the core of one of the two "founding peoples" of Canada, the other being the French Catholics of Lower Canada (now known as Quebec). Of course, the English Protestant versus French Catholic conflict has been a central theme of Canadian history.

Anyway, a powerful Protestant fraternal organization called the Orange Order gathered a large membership in Upper Canada (i.e., Ontario), including several top political leaders. With this in mind, Avramenko says that Ontario developed what he calls the "Orangemen Consciousness." As the new Dominion of Canada expanded and acquired what is now Western Canada, this Orangeman Consciousness would essentially evolve into a concept of national identity.

However, the Orangeman Consciousness never really took hold in the West. First of all, the Métis under Louis Riel rebelled against the Canadian authorities. More importantly, however, a vast wave of new settlers from Eastern Europe was brought in to settle the prairies. As Avramenko writes,

> These were peasants deliberately recruited from Eastern Europe under the immigration policies of the then Minister of Interior, Clifford Sifton. It was Sifton who saw the great economic potential of a developed agricultural base in the West and therefore opened immigration offices in Eastern Europe with the express intention of finding peoples both hardy and desperate enough to resettle on the harsh prairie (Avramenko 2013, 59).

These "peasants" had no connection to the Orangeman Consciousness whatsoever. Furthermore, some people in Ontario considered the immigrants arriving in the West to be lesser beings. According to Avramenko,

> The view of the Orangeman towards the immigrants settling the West is summarized by the words of the Right Honorable Sir McKenzie Bowell, "The Galicians, they of the sheepskin coats, the filth and the vermin, do not make splendid material for the building of a great nation. One look at the disgusting creatures after they pass through over the CPR on their way West has caused many to marvel that beings bearing the human form could have sunk to such a bestial level" (Avramenko 2013, 49).

Interestingly, Avramenko sees this attitude towards the Eastern Europeans settling the prairies as the origin of anti-Western sentiment in Ontario. As he puts it, "This prejudice continues to this day in anti-Alberta rhetoric" (Avramenko 2013, 60).

Homestead Consciousness

Because the new settlers came directly to the West, bypassing any immersion into the Orangeman Consciousness, Westerners developed their own way of thinking, distinct from the inhabitants of Ontario and Eastern Canada. Avramenko calls this the "Homestead Consciousness." As he puts it, "In the West one finds what may provisionally be called the Homestead Consciousness. This consciousness, it must be recognized, is not merely a nuanced variation of the Orangeman consciousness. It is an altogether different way of thinking; consequently, it leads us to recognize a distinct society" (Avramenko 2013, 59).

He describes it this way: "The Homestead Consciousness is a way of thinking that accords with the landscape—with horizons of legitimacy and political authority based on the freedom, the self-reliance, and the rugged individualism both born of and necessary for the survival of a homesteader on the vast and unrelenting prairie" (Avramenko 2013,

59). In short, Westerners have developed a different sense of identity than Easterners.

The West is, therefore, a distinct society, but one that not everyone appreciates. Avramenko recounts that during the 2006 federal election the Ontario establishment trotted out infamous abortionist Henry Morgentaler to condemn the Alberta-led Conservative Party. The message conveyed in doing so was clear: "Not only do these Albertans dwell on a lower moral plane, they are like Americans." Furthermore, he adds, "During the same election, Bloc Quebecois leader Gilles Duceppe was less veiled in his anti-Alberta rhetoric, claiming that a vote for the Conservative party was to cede power to Calgary—it would be un-Canadian to vote for representation outside of the geopolitical sphere of the two founding peoples" (Avramenko 2013, 60).

In short, "pointing to the West, and Alberta in particular, as the enemy is de rigueur for Quebeckers as well" (Avramenko 2013, 60).

Two Roots of Anti-Albertanism

As Avramenko sees it, Anti-Albertanism is essentially rooted in two aspects of the Orangeman Consciousness: anti-Americanism and disdain for the original Eastern European prairie settlers. As he puts it, "Anti-Albertanism, not surprisingly, is predicated on the same identity-giving premise the Loyalists and Orangemen brought to Upper Canada: anti-Americanism. Americans, after all, are gun-toting, money-grubbing, selfish, religious nuts, are they not? Just like those Albertans" (Avramenko 2013, 61).

A residual and unconscious antipathy towards the early settlers is also apparent: "Anti-Albertanism thus has this ring: they are dirty, shtetl-dwelling, money-grubbing, peasants who pose a grave threat to the sanctity of our self-enclosed higher moral reality" (Avramenko 2013, 61).

Clearly, according to this account, many Easterners view Albertans as being different from them, and not in a good way. Their view of

Canadian identity is not inclusive of the Western experience. Even the Canadian maple leaf flag is unrepresentative of the West in the sense that the sugar maple does not grow in the West.

Avramenko's analysis includes much more than is described here, but he summarizes his main point as follows:

> To conclude, if we want to inquire into Alberta's political self-understanding, we must do this vis-à-vis the so-called problem of Canadian identity. This problem, however, is framed only within the narrative of the French-English/Catholic-Protestant conflict that ends long before the 100th meridian, where the great plains begin. The effort to construct a national identity based on problems descending from this conflict is inappropriate for the West. Albertans have an identity—an identity that might very well be symbolized by a cowboy hat. It is not an identity and tradition needing to be invented, nor one for which apology is needed (Avramenko 2013, 61-62).

Conclusion

When considering the historical development of Alberta and the Prairies, then, it is possible to conclude that the unique characteristics of this region make it a "distinct society" in some sense. In this light, Alberta's conflict with Central Canada is rooted in more than simply economic matters. Canada drains Alberta financially, of course, but Alberta's identity also differs from what has frequently been referred to as the "national identity."

So, if Alberta is exploited by and disrespected by Central Canada, what should it do? Many will answer that voting for the Conservative Party of Canada is the answer. With a Conservative federal government in Ottawa, Alberta's problems could be addressed and resolved. However, as the next chapter will demonstrate, there are good reasons to reject that proposed solution. The federal Conservative Party will always have an incentive to pursue votes in Central Canada at the expense of Alberta.

Chapter 5

THE CONSERVATIVE PARTY IS NOT THE SOLUTION

Throughout the 1970s, most Albertans realized that Prime Minister Pierre Trudeau was an adversary to their province. Therefore, they pinned their hopes on the Progressive Conservative Party of Canada to rescue them from unfair treatment by the federal Liberals. In 1979, the federal PCs won a minority government under Joe Clark, but it was short-lived, and Trudeau was soon back in power to continue his dirty work.

In 1983, Brian Mulroney became leader of the federal Tories. Trudeau resigned in 1984 and was replaced as Liberal leader by John Turner. In the September 1984 election, Mulroney won a landslide victory. He garnered almost 69 per cent of the popular vote in Alberta along with all 21 of the province's federal seats. He also won 58 of Quebec's 75 seats. It looked like smooth sailing for the West after more than a decade of Trudeau's blatant hostility.

But things weren't as good as they seemed. Mulroney's Quebec MPs outnumbered his Prairie MPs, and he was a Quebec MP himself. Quebec's influence would dramatically affect government decision-making, and not in a good way, for the West.

This was clearly seen when Mulroney's government had to decide whether to give a maintenance contract for the CF-18 fighter aircraft to the Winnipeg-based Bristol Aerospace Ltd., or to the Montreal-based Canadair Ltd. The companies' bids were compared on technical capability and price. Bristol came out ahead, scoring 926 out of 1000 points compared to Canadair's 843 points. Nevertheless, on October 31, 1986, the Mulroney government awarded the contract to Canadair.

The government claimed that its decision was based on the fact that Canadair would benefit more from the transfer of new technology than Bristol would. But this was rather fishy. As political scientists Robert M. Campbell and Leslie A. Pal note, Robert de Cotret, president of the Treasury Board, subsequently admitted "that the question of technology transfer had never been explicit in the original tender.... The government, in short, had based its decision on a criterion never advertised to bidders" (Campbell and Pal 1989, 33).

Not only that, but the technology transfer consideration was dubious at best.

> All of the technology would be transferred from McDonnell Douglas, and Bristol spokespersons argued that the giant American aerospace company would only license the technology for specific use on the CF-18. Bristol also claimed that its partners already had access to much of the technology through their parent companies (Campbell and Pal 1989, 35).

The Manitoba government agreed with this argument and added that Canadair would have to pay for the use of McDonnell Douglas technology, adding to the cost. "The province's position was confirmed the next day by the McDonnell Douglas corporation. A spokesperson said that any technology or data transferred by McDonnell Douglas would have to be purchased, and could not be applied or used on projects other than the CF-18" (Campbell and Pal 1989, 37).

Knowing this, Manitobans rejected the technology transfer argument as a ruse. The real reason for awarding the contract to Canadair, Westerners believed, was "that the Tories had looked at their sagging popularity in Quebec and decided to give the contract to Montreal to improve their election chances" (Campbell and Pal 1989, 43).

Many Westerners were understandably outraged by this event. Campbell and Pal write that, "The decision engendered a depth of bitterness not seen in the West since the energy wars over the National Energy Program. Life-time [Progressive Conservative] party members tore up their cards" (Campbell and Pal 1989, 35).

Preston Manning, in his 1992 book *The New Canada*, explained the implications clearly:

For many westerners, the CF-18 decision had the same odour as the NEP, only this policy was instituted not by the Liberals but by the new Conservative government, which was supposed to be introducing more regional fairness and balance into national decision making. The CF-18 decision also showed westerners exactly how much influence their PC members and cabinet ministers had in the new government when push came to shove. To add insult to injury, instead of sending de Cotret to Winnipeg to deliver the bad news, the government told Jake Epp, the senior cabinet minister from Manitoba, to explain to Manitobans how awarding the contract to Canadair instead of to Bristol was "in the national intertest" (Manning 1992, 127).

Yes, "the national interest." Whatever benefits Central Canada at the expense of the West, is in "the national interest." From this perspective, the West is simply an appendage of "the nation," there to support and help maintain it.

The point is, though, that Brian Mulroney's PC government was doing what any federal government would do – cater to the voters of Central Canada. That's where the majority of the votes are. Had the contract been awarded to Winnipeg, the Tories would have paid a political price in Quebec, which they wanted to avoid at all costs. This is basic Canadian political math. And it explains why voting for the Conservative Party of Canada will not solve Alberta's problems.

The national party calculation

The calculation faced by Mulroney's government is common to all federal parties in Canada. Central Canada has the majority of votes, so it ends up calling the shots regardless of any election outcome.

This situation is very well explained by University of Calgary professors Ted Morton, Tom Flanagan, and Jack Mintz. Having a Conservative government in Ottawa is, of course, better for Alberta than a Liberal government. However, it is at best a temporary solution: "Being part of a winning national majority government—the Mulroney government in 1980s, the Harper Government in the 2000s—may bring Alberta some short-term protection, but the *status quo ante* returns" (Morton, Flanagan, and Mintz 2020, 254-255).

At some point, the need to please Central Canada at the expense of the West (or at least at the expense of Alberta) will occur.

> The root cause is an electoral system that invites federal political parties to win voter majorities in Ontario and Quebec with policies that transfer wealth from Western Canada. Ontario (121) and Quebec (78) together have 199 MPs, well over the 170 seats required to form a majority government. In the absence of effective regional representation in an elected and equal Senate, the interests of the less populated provinces are always at risk of being marginalized. Historically, this has typically been the political strategy of the Liberal Party. But the same defect shapes the electoral strategies of conservative parties. Their typical base in Western Canada does not have enough MPs to form a majority government, so it too must be attentive to the central Canadian interests (Morton, Flanagan, and Mintz 2020, 255).

The political calculation involved is very simple: "Vote-seeking national political parties will seek to win elections by promising policies that redistribute wealth from regions with more wealth but fewer voters to regions that are less wealthy but have more voters" (Morton, Flanagan, and Mintz 2020, 256).

From an historical perspective, Roger Gibbins and Loleen Berdahl explain the failure of the West to achieve reform through political parties:

> The partisan history of western Canada offers little hope that the party system, in whole or in its specific parts, will provide a vehicle for addressing either western alienation or regional aspirations. The party system has been more the source of regional discontent than a vehicle through which discontent might be addressed or moderated. Western-based parties — the Progressive Party of Canada, Social Credit, the CCF, the Reform Party of Canada, and the Canadian Alliance — have failed to win national power, and even national influence has been questionable. The Reform Party's clarion call that "the West wants in" was widely derided outside the West as narrow regionalism unsuitable to a truly national party, although

"Quebec wants in" has been the informal federalist mantra for
generations, and "Ontario is in" is a fact of life. The historical
lesson is that western-based parties do not win national office,
and national parties explicitly appealing to western regional
interests are rare. Indeed, the party system has helped define
"regional" in the case of the West, and the West alone, as
somehow antithetical to "national." Parties based largely in
Ontario and Quebec are self-defined as national, a definition
generally accepted by the media and elite political discourse.
Parties based largely in the West are defined, and defined
successfully by their opponents and the media, as regional. The
West is the only Canadian region earmarked in this fashion and
the only region with interests assumed to be at odds with the
national interest, whatever that might be (Gibbins and Berdahl
2003, 110-111).

Clearly, this suggests that trying to improve the West's situation within
Canada through a national political party is hopeless.

The Conservative Party leadership selection process

Besides the inevitable challenges Westerners face in convincing the
Conservative Party to embrace policies favourable to the West, they
also encounter obstacles for influence within the Conservative Party
itself.

Ontario MP Erin O'Toole was elected the new leader of the
Conservative Party of Canada (CPC) on August 23, 2020. Many
of the best people in Alberta and the other Western provinces were
actively engaged in the leadership selection process. Much was at
stake because almost every Member of Parliament in Alberta and
Saskatchewan is from the CPC, and it is perceived to be the best
federal party to represent the West. But how many people remember
that the leadership selection process adopted by the CPC was
deliberately designed to thwart its Western base?

When the Canadian Alliance under Stephen Harper and Progressive
Conservative Party of Canada under Peter MacKay were negotiating
a merger in 2003, the leadership selection process was a key point
of contention. The Canadian Alliance had a "one member, one vote"
system. The PCs under Peter MacKay absolutely refused to accept

that system, because the large number of members in the West would dominate the new party. The Tories would never agree to form a new political party that would be predominantly controlled by Westerners.

The PCs developed a scheme to overcome the perceived Western problem. As John Ibbitson wrote,

> the Tories proposed a system in which each member of the new party would cast a vote within his or her own riding. Each riding would be awarded a hundred points. If one candidate received 60 per cent of the vote in that riding, he or she would score sixty points in that riding. This meant that a riding in, say, northern Quebec, where only ten votes were cast, would have the same weight as a Calgary riding where thousands of votes were cast. On the one hand, the system would be less democratic; on the other, candidates would be forced to run a truly national campaign. And a candidate from the Progressive Conservative side of the party – Peter MacKay, for instance – would at least have a chance (Ibbitson 2015, 177).

At first, Harper rejected that idea. Harper then suggested compromise proposals, but MacKay refused to budge. So how was a deal reached? Harper gave in. Ibbitson explained that,

> In essence, Harper had caved on everything. Leadership selection, convention votes – the Tories could have it all their way. MacKay was left with absolutely nothing to object to. If Paris was worth a mass, Harper had decided, acquiring the Progressive Conservatives was worth any concession he had to make (Ibbitson 2015, 178).

Henry IV had said that "Paris is worth a mass" when he saw that making an opportunistic change in his religious beliefs would enable him to obtain the French crown in 1593. In other words, the phrase justifies a sell-out for political gain.

Of course, the leadership selection process demanded by Peter MacKay is exactly what was used to select Erin O'Toole.

As Ibbitson pointed out, this means that – theoretically, at least – a Quebec riding with ten votes in the leadership contest carries the same weight as an Alberta riding with thousands of votes. How is that fair to Alberta or the West? It's not.

In 2020 there weren't any Quebec ridings with ten members outweighing Alberta ridings with thousands, but the disproportion was nevertheless very evident. Fifty ridings in Quebec contributed less than 100 votes each in the leadership contest, with the Bourassa riding registering just 28. In contrast, 24 ridings in Alberta had over 1000 votes each, with the Foothills riding registering 2079. Clearly, Quebec's small CPC membership vastly outweighed Alberta's large CPC membership in the leadership selection process. Alberta's tremendous conservative strength was marginalized to a great extent.

The CPC's leadership selection process was deliberately designed to provide an institutional mechanism to thwart Western influence within the party. How can a party with this sort of built-in unfairness to the West properly represent Western interests?

At the CPC's national convention on March 19, 2021, delegates voted to modify the leadership selection rules "so that a riding with fewer than 100 votes will only get as many points in the leadership tally as votes cast" (Platt 2021a, A4). A riding with 50 members will only get 50 points, for example. Still, a Quebec riding with 100 members will have equal weight to an Alberta riding of 2000 members. The disparity is slightly reduced from the previous method, but Alberta will continue to be greatly disadvantaged in the process.

As it is, the new CPC leader has done nothing to dispel fears that his primary focus is on Central Canada. Indeed, as *Maclean's* columnist Paul Wells wrote recently, "O'Toole represents an attempt to put a more Ontario-friendly face forward, which means a blander face" (Wells 2021, 22).

There are other reasons to be concerned about O'Toole as well. He seems to be a chameleon who changes his colours depending on the situation. As Wells elaborates:

> Honestly, the difference between the personality O'Toole presented to Conservative members in the leadership race and the personality he's presenting to Canadians as a federal election approaches is spectacular. He was the True Blue

candidate who'd Take Canada Back. When Peter MacKay tried to get social-conservative gadfly Derek Sloan kicked out of the Conservative caucus, O'Toole blocked the effort and ran online ads to brag about it. Months later, as leader, he led the successful effort to get Sloan thrown out (Wells 2021, 23).

O'Toole presented himself as the genuine conservative "true blue" candidate during the CPC leadership contest, but quickly shifted to the political centre immediately after winning. Westerners cannot trust a politician whose positions change so readily and unexpectedly.

Conclusion

Erin O'Toole will undoubtedly make some noise about the need to address "Western alienation" to shore up support in the West. But all of Alberta's MPs save one, and all of Saskatchewan's, are already Conservative, so he will be focusing on ways to win seats in places like Toronto. This is the inevitable consequence of the current political structure and - as always – it will lead to the West taking a back seat to Central Canada in the electoral calculations of the CPC.

The CPC already subordinates Western interests to Eastern interests in its own leadership selection process, so doing the same when developing policy and an electoral strategy will come naturally.

The solution Alberta needs is not electing the CPC to form the government, but a referendum on independence. The legitimacy of this option will be covered in the next chapter.

Chapter 6

THE CONSTITUTIONAL PATH TO SECESSION

Sentiment in favour of secession was running strong in Alberta after the October 21, 2019 federal election that saw Justin Trudeau returned to power with a minority government. To deal with the anger felt in many parts of the province, Premier Jason Kenney launched a Fair Deal Panel to gather input from citizens about how Alberta could improve its situation within Canada.

On June 17, 2020, the official report of the Panel was made public. It recognized the widespread anger of Albertans towards the federal government. In response, the panel recommended a number of measures to reassert Alberta's jurisdictional powers within Canada, and to try to renegotiate the equalization program with the federal government and the other provinces.

Ted Morton, Tom Flanagan, and Jack Mintz refer to proposals for Alberta to exercise a greater degree of its existing constitutional powers as the "autonomist option." They view this option favourably, but also point out its limitations, namely, "autonomism does not directly address Alberta's most important problems" (Morton, Flanagan, and Mintz 2020, 271).

Nevertheless, implementing the kinds of policies advocated by autonomist supporters would clearly be beneficial were Alberta to move towards independence:

> The autonomist option could be helpful preparation for some version of separatism if Alberta is forced to move in that direction. For example, an Alberta police force could serve as the interim nucleus of an Alberta defence force while the

province was constructing a military appropriate to its needs. Likewise, the ability to directly collect provincial taxes would facilitate the transition to a national system of tax collection, as would provincial management of the health care system in its own sphere. In general, the more autonomous Alberta becomes, the easier it will be to contemplate full-fledged separation (Morton, Flanagan, and Mintz 2020, 270).

The Fair Deal Panel itself, though, was clear that it completely ruled out any consideration of Alberta independence, even as a last resort. The report acknowledged, "Some Albertans believe that the only way to get Ottawa and other provinces to pay attention to unfairness and misunderstandings is to use the threat of separation, implying that if Alberta does not get a fairer place within the federation, the province will pursue secession from Canada." (Fair Deal Panel 2020, 8). However, it quickly dismisses that option by stating: "But we do not believe the threat of secession is a constructive negotiating strategy." (Fair Deal Panel 2020, 8).

One panel member, MLA Drew Barnes, sent a letter to Premier Kenney publicly disagreeing with that conclusion. Barnes wrote, "While I appreciate that my colleagues on the panel do not believe that Alberta can or should raise the prospect of independence under any circumstance, I must respectfully disagree. A free people must be willing to at some point of injustice without rectification, to draw a line and make a stand" (Barnes 2020, 3).

Barnes' position is much like that of Ted Byfield, the influential publisher of *Alberta Report* magazine. Early in 2001, in the aftermath of the 2000 federal election, Byfield wrote columns explaining that only the threat of Alberta secession would make Central Canada take the province's concerns seriously.

In November 2000, Jean Chrétien's Liberals handily beat the Canadian Alliance, leaving a large number of Albertans unhappy with their province's status within Canada. Many wanted substantial change.

It was within this context that the famous "Firewall Letter," written by Stephen Harper and other prominent Albertans, was published. In a sense, that letter was a precursor to the Fair Deal Panel's report. It proposed that the Alberta government maximize its use of the province's constitutional powers, including collecting income tax, creating a provincial police force, initiating a provincial pension plan, and forcing Senate reform back onto the national agenda.

Byfield found the Firewall Letter to be defective on at least one point – there was no threat to back it up. In a January, 2001 column for *The Report* magazine, Byfield wrote:

> If Mr. Harper thinks that Alberta can merely proceed to exercise the same autonomy Quebec now does, he is dreaming. Quebec is a special case; it is, we are constantly told, "distinct." What makes it special? Its language? Its cultural heritage? Yes, but it always had those, and nobody outside Quebec gave a damn. Such autonomy as Quebec possesses was achieved in just one way: it made convincing threats to leave (Byfield 2001a, 68).

"The lesson is plain," Byfield continued. "If you really want change," he wrote, you must "threaten to leave—*and mean it*. Period. If we fail to understand this, we are not being patriotic. We are being stupid. Crassly, arrogantly, blindly stupid" (Byfield 2001a, 68).

He resumed this theme in a subsequent column with a title that said it all: "The West's paradox—the only way we can change Canada is by finding ways to leave it."

In this column Byfield made his argument forcefully:

> Unless we make credible threats to set up on our own we will get absolutely nothing by way of constitutional change, or any other kind of change. We will be bashed down every time. If we threatened to leave and meant it, we would have enormous clout in Canada, more even than Quebec. By refusing to entertain such an idea, we have no clout whatever. That is the message of history—and of the last three federal elections (Byfield 2001b, 60).

A message - one might add - overlooked by the Fair Deal Panel.

Byfield went on to argue that Alberta needed to explore alternatives to being in Canada, such as becoming an independent country or joining the United States. Once it was understood that these were viable options, Alberta could then return to the negotiating table to discuss its place within Canada. He wrote,

> We should go back to the negotiating table, just as Quebec is proposing to do, and we should go back as Quebec goes back—with other options clearly in view—such as an independent state, or joining the American union. If we go to the table with these alternatives thoroughly explored, tenable and widely understood, we will come away with quite a bit, and a very new Canada will emerge. If we go to the table without those options, we will come away with nothing whatever. All central Canada need do is stymie the negotiational process and we will have to slump back into the status quo as we always have (Byfield 2001b, 60).

Without practical alternatives, there is no reason why Central Canada would agree to any changes favourable to Alberta.

Byfield referred to Alberta's situation as "a paradox" because the "only way we can change Canada is to develop ways of getting out of Canada. We must possess other options" (Byfield 2001b, 60). This is undoubtedly true. By ruling out secession from the start, the Fair Deal Panel has thrown away Alberta's only significant alternative to the status quo. Drew Barnes is absolutely right – if Albertans cannot obtain significant changes within Canada, then "we must seek another relationship, as a sovereign people" (Barnes 2020, 3).

Almost 20 years after Byfield's columns, Flanagan, Mintz, and Morton came to a similar conclusion. In the final chapter of their book *Moment of Truth* they wrote:

> To repeat, none of us favor separation as a first option. But we also see it as a viable last resort if all else fails. It may be that in order to stay in Canada, Alberta must be able and willing to leave it. Otherwise, our grievances—our request for a fair deal—will never be taken seriously. Asking Ottawa and the rest of Canada to be "fair" to Alberta has not worked and will never work. For political change of this scale, appeals to fairness do not work. We must make the rest of Canada see

that it is in their self-interest to keep Alberta in Canada for the
contributions we make (Flanagan, Mintz, Morton 2020, 278).

Sounding very much like Byfield, they conclude, "This may be
Alberta's paradox: That we need to go half-way down a road to
a destination that we don't want, in order to get the policy and
constitutional changes necessary to stay in a Canada we love"
(Flanagan, Mintz, Morton 2020, 278).

Unlike those esteemed gentlemen, however, I do favour independence
as the first option. Alberta's concerns have been ignored and will
continue to be ignored. Self-determination will allow Albertans to
choose a better path towards continued economic development and
prosperity. The pathway to achieving self-determination has been
opened by the Supreme Court of Canada.

The constitutional legitimacy of Alberta's path to independence

The federal and provincial governments have the option of
submitting questions to the courts for advisory opinions on important
constitutional matters. In the aftermath of the 1995 Quebec referendum
on separation, Jean Chrétien's Liberal government asked the Supreme
Court of Canada about the legality of Quebec seceding unilaterally
from Canada. The Court's decision, issued in 1998, may turn out to
play a key role in Alberta's future. This ruling, known as Reference Re
Secession of Quebec, pioneered a constitutional path for provinces to
secede from Canada. That is to say, it established certain constitutional
principles that provide the foundation for the legitimacy of secession.

In their decision, the Supreme Court justices referred at least two times
to a "right" to pursue secession. In the first instance they state, "The
rights of other provinces and the federal government cannot deny the
right of the government of Quebec to pursue secession, should a clear
majority of the people of Quebec choose that goal, so long as in doing
so, Quebec respects the rights of others" ([1998] 2 S.C.R. 267).

Later, they essentially make the same point: "The other provinces and
the federal government would have no basis to deny the right of the
government of Quebec to pursue secession, should a clear majority of
the people of Quebec choose that goal, so long as in doing so, Quebec
respects the rights of others" ([1998] 2 S.C.R. 293-294).

Ultimately, however, the key conclusion reached by the court was that "a clear majority vote in Quebec on a clear question in favour of secession would confer democratic legitimacy on the secession initiative which all of the other participants in Confederation would have to recognize" ([1998] 2 S.C.R. 293).

This is the main point to understand, namely, that if a "clear majority" votes "on a clear question in favour of secession," a province has the "democratic legitimacy" necessary to leave Confederation, although the details must be negotiated with other key parties, especially the federal government.

Following the Court's decision, constitutional scholars across Canada wrote about its significance. Ted Morton emphasized its originality:

> Here, for the first time ever, the Supreme Court has created (it certainly can't be found anywhere in the text of the Constitution) a constitutional "right to pursue secession." And of course, where there are rights, there are corollary duties. And so the Court goes on to tell us that if the separatists were to win a referendum "by a clear majority on a clear question," then Canada has a "constitutional duty to negotiate." Indeed, the Court goes on to say that there is corollary obligation to negotiate in "good faith" (Morton 1999, 121).

Morton summarized the situation this way: "As of August 1998, Quebec now has, in writing, a 'constitutional right' to pursue secession and Canada has a 'constitutional duty to negotiate'" (Morton 1999, 121).

Much like Morton, José Woehrling, a law professor at the University of Montreal, pointed out that secession had become clearly constitutional for the first time. As he explained,

> the Court proclaims the "democratic legitimacy" of a secession initiative approved by a clear majority vote in Quebec on a clear question. In the past, certain commentators in the rest of Canada have affirmed that the mere attempt to separate Quebec from Canada was illegitimate and even illegal. Such arguments have now been put to rest (Woehrling 1999, 125).

In the aftermath of the *Secession Reference* case, the federal government passed the *Clarity Act* to spell out the process that a province would need to follow in order to properly secede from Canada. However, a number of scholars in Quebec believe that the *Clarity Act* is much more stringent than necessary. They see it as creating needlessly difficult hurdles for a seceding province to follow (Dumberry 2006, 448).

However, it's unlikely that those hurdles could effectively block a legitimate effort towards provincial independence. As Patrick Dumberry, a law professor at the University of Ottawa, has written,

> to the extent that a referendum would result in the clear expression by the people of Quebec of their will to secede from Canada, the unwillingness of the federal government to undertake negotiations, or even the interdiction to do so under the Clarity Act, would not prevent Quebec from eventually becoming an independent State (Dumberry 2006, 452).

According to Dumberry, the democratic will of a citizenry expressed through a referendum takes precedence over any significant obstacles that the federal government may use to block an attempt at secession. In short, if a clear majority of voters in one province supported a clear question on secession from Canada, the federal government would have a hard time blocking that province from seceding.

Occasionally, people who supported efforts for provincial independence were accused of being "traitors." However, when the Supreme Court of Canada determines that provincial secession is legitimate (albeit under certain conditions), it is impossible that such a course could be considered "treason." Acting in accordance with the supreme law of the land could never be considered treasonous.

This point was made by Jacques-Yvan Morin, a law professor at the University of Montreal. As he explained, the *Secession Reference* case "finally puts to rest the opinion heard now and again—unfortunately from the mouths of more than one English Canadian jurist—suggesting that any attempt to promote sovereignty constitutes treason" (Morin 1999, 117).

More recent scholarship also recognizes the legitimacy of provincial secession. The most significant for Alberta is an article by Richard Albert, a Canadian who is a law professor at the University of Texas at Austin. He is opposed to Alberta seceding from Canada, but he is a democrat who recognizes that provinces have the right to self-determination and that Canadian constitutional law allows for such:

> But as wrong and regrettable as Alberta's secession would be, the choice should nevertheless be open to Albertans. Democracy demands nothing less than the free, fair, and informed power of choice. The fundamental promise of democracy is that the people should have the power to chart their own path, whether that means how to restructure their government, what powers should be delegated to their representatives, and when their Constitution should be revised to reflect new values. No democracy should ever deny the people the right to make a properly considered decision about self-government. All options should be available, even the choice to make a wrong turn (Albert 2020, 193).

Albert mentions that throughout history, many instances of secession have involved violence. However, in Canada, such an unhappy outcome is unnecessary to achieve provincial independence. That's because there is a constitutional process for it laid out in the *Secession Reference* case, "a judgment that applies today not only to Quebec but to all provinces that may have a valid claim to secession" (Albert 2020, 194).

Therefore, "Were Alberta to hold an unarguably deliberative, fair, and informed referendum on secession, it would be difficult to deny the validity of the outcome of the vote" (Albert 2020, 197).

The Alberta government has the authority to hold a referendum on secession from Canada. Doing so would enable Albertans to make a choice about their future. If the provincial government refuses to hold such a referendum, Albertans can elect a new government that will give them one.

Alberta independence, not Americanization

Among those who favour Alberta leaving Canada are some who think that Alberta should join the United States. This position is most prominently presented in a book by American geopolitical strategist Peter Zeihan entitled, *The Accidental Superpower: The Next Generation of American Preeminence and the Coming Global Disorder*.

The main thrust of the book is to explain why the United States is a major world power as a result of geopolitical factors. However, it received some Canadian media attention because of its chapter about Alberta. Zeihan demonstrates that Alberta is paying much more than its fair share in Canada and that it will increasingly pay more in the years ahead. In his view, this continual transfer of wealth from Alberta to central Canada will lead to pressure for Alberta to separate.

Zeihan points out that in 2012, Alberta paid $16 billion more into Canada than it received. Over time, Alberta's contribution will increase and become even more disproportionate. He writes,

> As the demographic and financial disconnect between Alberta and the rest of Canada grows, these younger, more highly skilled, and better-paid Albertan's will be forced to pay ever higher volumes of taxes to Ottawa to compensate for increasingly older, less skilled, and lower-income Canadians elsewhere in the country. Plagued by rafts of elderly Canadians who are no longer paying into the system but instead drawing out, the net per capita Albertan tax bill is likely to breach $20,000 by 2020 (Zeihan 2014, 259-260).

That prediction was wrong, of course, but his key point is correct: "Economic and political trends are pushing Alberta out of the Canadian mainstream just as surely as they are sucking it dry" (Zeihan 2014, 266).

Zeihan believes that Alberta would be much better off if it separated from Canada. However, he does not think it should become an independent country. He writes, "While Alberta would do much better if it were not part of Canada, it would not do better as an independent country" (Zeihan 2014, 263). Instead, he thinks Alberta should join the United States. In his view, doing so would solve many of Alberta's problems and bring it significant economic advantages.

However, Zeihan does not appear to have considered some significant political factors. Most importantly, if Alberta were to join the United States, it would immediately lose some of the powers it already exercises within Canada. State governments have much less power within the US than provinces have within Canada.

Roger Gibbins made this point decades ago. The weakness of the individual states is reflected in the respective powers of American governors versus Canadian premiers. As Gibbins points out, "When governors go to Washington they take with them less power than do Canadian premiers" (Gibbins 1982, 107).

The American system was originally designed to be decentralized and to provide considerable power to the states. However, over time, and especially after the Civil War, the US federal government dramatically extended its power at the expense of the states.

Some of this transfer of power from the states to the national government has resulted from the success of the American system in representing local interests within federal institutions. Gibbins explains as follows:

> It must be emphasized that success at handling territorial conflict has facilitated the nationalization of American politics, and has strengthened the national government vis-à-vis the states. Effective territorial representation within national political institutions has promoted national integration, strengthened the national government, broadened its reach, and reduced the power of the state governments to a degree unimagined in the founding years of the American republic (Gibbins 1982, 195).

Look at that last part very carefully: "strengthened the national government, broadened its reach, and reduced the power of the state governments to a degree unimagined in the founding years of the American republic." The strengthening of federal power and reduction of state power has probably continued since Gibbins wrote those words in 1982. If Alberta joined the US, it would soon suffer under the overwhelming rule of Washington, with no recourse.

Conclusion

If Albertans want to control their own destiny, they must choose independence. The Supreme Court of Canada has created a constitutional pathway for provinces to secede from the country. A clear majority voting in favour of independence on a clear question provides a province with the democratic legitimacy needed to pursue self-determination. By becoming independent in this manner, Alberta could solve many of the economic problems imposed on it by Ottawa.

Joining the United States, on the other hand, would result in Alberta being suffocated by a powerful central government based in Washington, DC. Alberta's future would be in the hands of a distant and uncaring political establishment. Independence could improve Alberta's current situation, but becoming part of the United States would likely only make things worse.

Chapter 7

THE INDEPENDENCE MOVEMENT TODAY

As long as Stephen Harper was prime minister of Canada, there wasn't much room for an independence movement in Alberta. Harper was well-known as a friend of Alberta, as his co-authorship of the Firewall Letter had demonstrated.

During Harper's term in office, the only recognizable manifestation of secessionism was the tiny Separation Party of Alberta. In all three of the provincial elections that occurred while Harper was in power (2008, 2012, and 2015), the party ran only one candidate. In 2008, its candidate received a little over 100 votes, but in the subsequent two elections he received less than 100 votes. Clearly, the party was barely alive. The Separation Party changed its name to the Alberta First Party in 2013, and ran under that name in the 2015 election.

The political landscape changed dramatically later in 2015 when the Liberal Party won the federal election and Justin Trudeau became prime minister. Suddenly, a number of independence-oriented Facebook pages appeared and quickly gathered thousands of members. The Facebook activity indicated only a superficial level of commitment to the cause, but it demonstrated that many people had become open to the independence option. In the following few years, public discussion of secession became increasingly common.

With growing support for independence becoming more apparent, the Alberta First Party changed its name to the Freedom Conservative Party of Alberta in 2018. Independent MLA Derek Fildebrandt joined the party and became its leader.

By December 2018, talk of the secession option was flooding the media. In the *Financial Post*, Lawrence Solomon warned that those who saw Alberta's landlocked position as an insurmountable barrier to independence had things backwards:

> An independent Alberta would control access to its land
> mass as well as the skies above it, requiring Canada's federal
> government to negotiate rights for, say, Vancouver-to-Toronto
> flights over Alberta airspace. Canada would also need Alberta's
> agreement to have trains and trucks cross its now-international
> borders. Threats of tolls and tariffs could abound as needed
> to chasten those perceived to be wronging Alberta, whether
> Quebec, which exports dairy to B.C., grain interests that now
> commandeer rail to the detriment of Alberta's oil shippers, or
> the B.C. ports that depend on commodities going to and from
> points east. Anyone thinking that Alberta would be unable to
> police its borders needs to be reminded that, for the past 70
> years, Alberta's patrols have made it the continent's only rat-
> free jurisdiction (Solomon 2018, FP9).

Calgary businessman W. Brett Wilson, a former Dragon's Den star, publicly expressed some sympathy towards secession. "My belief is we're being pushed out of Confederation," he told *Calgary Herald* columnist Don Braid. Wilson further explained,

> I'm not a separatist. I'm a frustrated nationalist who doesn't
> believe Confederation as designed is working in our favour.
> My first choice is to renegotiate Confederation. My second
> choice is to leave Confederation. But I'm not leading that
> charge. I'm saying, "hey guys, I want to renegotiate our place
> in Canada" (Braid 2018, A6).

At about the same time, *Edmonton Journal* columnist David Staples wrote about the widespread interest in independence:

> It's now common for Albertans on social media to raise the
> issue of separation. There's no official separatist party, but if
> other provinces continue to enjoy tens of billions in benefits
> that annually flow from Alberta's oil economy, yet refuse to
> allow necessary pipeline infrastructure, the anger and alarm in
> Alberta will explode into a populist movement (Staples 2018,
> A2).

Senator Doug Black told Staples that everywhere he went in Alberta he heard people discussing separation. He had the same experience while being a guest on an Edmonton talk radio show. Black said that's what the callers wanted to talk about: "How does Alberta separate? When do we separate? I get it everywhere. I think that's the wrong way to go, but quite clearly it's time for a business conversation about our relationship with Canada" (Staples 2018, A2).

Shortly thereafter, Jack Mintz weighed in on "Albexit" in the pages of the *Financial Post*. Mintz pointed to the obvious foolishness of the keep-it-in-the-ground crowd who want to shut down Alberta's fossil fuel industry:

> The possibility of leaving Alberta oil wealth in the ground, while world demand — already at 100 million barrels per day — keeps growing at a robust 1.5 per cent each year, is an existential threat to the province. Despite endless promises from so many self-appointed prophets of a renewable future, demand for oil continues to rise since it is needed for petrochemicals (such as all those plastics in all our tech gadgets) as well as air, sea, rail and short- and long-haul road transport. Even with rising production of electric vehicles, all the credible energy agencies project that demand for oil in 2050 will be as high as or higher than demand today (Mintz 2018, FP11).

Mintz went on to point out that despite this worldwide demand for oil,

> Alberta is looking at being forced to sit it out, thanks to political decisions being made by Canadians outside the province. Because of the lack of pipeline capacity promoted by environmentalists who push for Canada to be a "climate leader," and the politicians who play along, Albertans are losing high-paying jobs, wealth, government revenues and foreign investment in the oil patch. The lack of support from other provinces — especially British Columbia and Quebec — is raising questions about Alberta's place in Confederation. Quebec's premier, François Legault, recently called Alberta's oil "dirty energy" and said he doesn't want it piped through his province, even as Quebec imports substantial volumes of

that supposedly undesirable Alberta oil through Enbridge Line 9. Albertans can't help but wonder why they should stand for being slapped in the face after the federal government, Quebec and the rest of Canada have been happy to take the hundreds of billions of dollars that Albertans and their "dirty" oil have provided them over the decades (Mintz 2018, FP11).

Mintz then drew the logical conclusion that ongoing opposition to Alberta's oil industry was making the independence of the province an increasing possibility:

> It's typical to pooh-pooh the possibility of Alberta separation as unrealistic, given the close familial and economic relationships Albertans have with other parts of Canada. But if Brexit happened, then Albexit is just as possible. Probably more so, given the existential threat to Alberta's prosperity over resource development (Mintz 2018, FP11).

Political developments

The widespread discussion about secession began to impact the political scene. Toward the end of 2018, the Freedom Conservative Party unveiled its 2019 election platform. A major thrust of the platform was that within one year of the provincial election, Ottawa must grant a fair deal for Alberta within Canada, or the province would hold an independence referendum. Party leader Derek Fildebrandt was quoted as saying, "I do not believe independence is the answer today, but the status quo is unacceptable and merely complaining about it is not enough. . . . Canada is worth trying to save, but we should not stay at any price" (Graney 2018, 6).

The Freedom Conservative Party was offering Canada one last chance to address Alberta's grievances. If that was not forthcoming, Albertans would be given the opportunity to vote for independence.

A few weeks later, a more explicitly secessionist party was registered, the Alberta Independence Party led by Dave Bjorkman. As one source put it, "The Alberta Independence Party has enjoyed something of a meteoric rise. A year ago, it was a jumbled group with assorted ideas. Now it has 63 candidates — 12 more than the Alberta Liberals — and official party status" (Graney 2019, A2).

Alberta's next provincial election was held on April 16, 2019. The Freedom Conservative Party ran 24 candidates and received 0.52 percent of the provincial vote. The Alberta Independence Party ran 63 candidates and received 0.71 percent of the vote. The small vote totals for these parties were at least partly a reflection of the polarized political situation within the province. Most people saw voting for the United Conservative Party (UCP) under Jason Kenney as the only way to unseat the unpopular NDP government of Rachel Notley.

Wexit

In January 2019, former RCMP officer Peter Downing created an organization called Alberta Fights Back. In February it put up billboards in Calgary and Edmonton asking, "Should Alberta Ditch Canada?" That led to a similar campaign in Regina and Saskatoon asking, "Should Saskatchewan Leave Canada?" Subsequently, Downing created an organization called Wexit with plans to register a provincial and federal political party under that name.

On October 21, 2019, Canada held a federal election in which Justin Trudeau was re-elected with a minority government. Although Alberta had voted 69 percent for the Conservatives and Saskatchewan had voted 64 percent for the Conservatives, the Liberals topped the polls in Ontario and Quebec, thereby winning enough seats to keep them in power.

Anger in Alberta over the reelection of the Liberals was intense. As Ted Morton wrote days after the election, "Our news media is flooded with stories about the tsunami of separatist sentiment that has exploded in Western Canada since Monday's federal election. Memberships for a 'WEXIT' website soared from 2,500 to 125,000 in less than 24 hours. Signatures on an online petition to separate have surpassed 80,000 and more are being added every minute" (Morton 2019, A17).

With feelings running high, Peter Downing held three Wexit meetings during November. The Edmonton event was attended by at least 700 people, the Calgary event had as many as 1700 people, and the Red

Deer event about 700 people. Clearly, the movement was growing rapidly.

A major national magazine published an article on the Wexit movement noting, "A referendum on Alberta's relationship with the rest of the country feels practically inevitable at this point" (Fawcett 2020, 29).

On February 20, 2020, four Conservative MPs from Alberta issued a manifesto called The Buffalo Declaration that outlined Alberta's grievances with Canada and demanded positive change. As Don Braid noted in the *National Post*, "The declaration is strong, but it does not — as critics already allege — advocate Alberta separation. The substantial document argues that serious structural change is needed, far beyond mere politics, to accommodate Alberta within Confederation in a healthy way" (Braid 2020, A10). He further noted that, "Alberta is truly on the boil, with more grievances to come. At its heart, the declaration captures the seething alienation that regularly shows up as separatist support in polls" (Braid 2020, A10).

In April 2020, Wexit Alberta and the Freedom Conservative Party agreed to merge to form one party. Members of both groups approved the merger on June 29, under the name, Wildrose Independence Party of Alberta (WIPA). Paul Hinman, a former MLA, was named the interim leader.

In the meantime, the Alberta Independence Party changed its name to the Independence Party of Alberta.

Additionally, Peter Downing began creating a federal party, Wexit Canada, in January 2020. In June he resigned as leader and was replaced by former Conservative Party MP, Jay Hill. In September, Wexit Canada changed its name to the Maverick Party, with plans to run candidates in the next federal election.

At the time of writing, this is essentially where things stand.

Conclusion

Since the election of Justin Trudeau in 2015, the Alberta independence movement has been growing and organizing. At this point, there have been no electoral successes, but they could be just around the corner. Another victory by Justin Trudeau in the next federal election, which is expected this year (2021), will likely generate more support for Alberta independence than ever before. The future of the movement looks bright.

Conclusion

In a speech delivered during the 1935 provincial election campaign, soon-to-be premier William Aberhart famously stated: "If you have not suffered enough, it is your God-given right to suffer more" (Irving 1959, 291).

That statement equally applies to Alberta's current situation. If Albertans are satisfied that they can survive the economic calamity that will result from federal government climate change policies, they can choose to remain in Canada and suffer the consequences. If, however, they aspire to economic prosperity for themselves and their children, they should choose to form a new country in Western Canada.

The purpose of this book has been to argue that Alberta needs to exercise its right to self-determination. Currently, with key decisions about Alberta's future being made in Ottawa, and in the best interests of Central Canada, its future is in jeopardy. Albertans must make those decisions themselves if they want a free and prosperous future.

It is this need for self-determination that provides the crux of the argument for independence:

> The strongest argument for separation is that the province would have more ability to determine its own destiny. The billions in net fiscal transfers to the rest of country [sic] would be money kept by the province for its own affairs. Alberta would have full control over resource development and be able to negotiate its own trade and security agreements with the United States, Canada, and other countries (Flanagan, Mintz, and Morton 2020, 272).

Not only is self-determination necessary, but Canadian constitutional law allows for provinces to leave the federation in a peaceful manner. It's time to go.

Small-c conservative perspective

Historically, supporters of Alberta's independence movement have been grounded in small-c conservative thinking that values free enterprise, private property, the traditional family, and the historic virtues of Western civilization. That is, after all, Alberta's heritage.

The kind of broad-based conservative perspective that is needed for Alberta was exemplified by the Reform Party of Canada. That party began as a clear manifestation of Western regional sentiment. It was very popular in Alberta, garnering over 52 percent of the provincial vote in the 1993 federal election, and over 54 percent in the 1997 federal election.

Among the Statement of Principles approved at the party's founding convention in 1987 are the following points that clearly identify the party as conservative:

> 5. We affirm the value and dignity of the *individual person*, and the importance of strengthening and protecting the *family unit* as essential to the wellbeing of individuals and society. . . . 7. We believe in the value of *enterprise and initiative*, and that governments have a responsibility to foster and protect an environment in which initiative and enterprise can be exercised by individuals and groups. 8. We believe that the creation of wealth and productive jobs for Canadians is best achieved through the operations of a *responsible, broadly-based, free-enterprise economy* in which private property, freedom of contract, and the operations of free markets are encouraged and respected (Reform Party of Canada 1988, 26).

The goals of the independence movement are self-determination and greater freedom for Alberta, and these goals only make sense from a small-c conservative perspective.

A charismatic leader is needed

So, what will it take to galvanize an effective independence movement in Alberta? Needless to say, a number of elements are necessary for any political movement, including organizations, committed supporters, and financial resources. However, a particular kind of charismatic and high-energy leader is likely essential for taking the independence movement to the next level. The necessity of dynamic leadership for building a new political movement is commonly seen in history, especially from Alberta's own history.

In Alberta, the most striking example of indispensable leadership would be that of William Aberhart and the Social Credit Party. Aberhart was the principal of Crescent Heights High School in Calgary and a popular Bible teacher. As a pioneer radio evangelist, he had amassed a very large and loyal audience throughout Alberta. However, Aberhart was not active in politics until one of his favourite Grade 12 students committed suicide in 1932 due to hardships resulting from the Great Depression. After that heartrending event, he read a book about Social Credit theory, which he found convincing.

Aberhart then began to use his religious broadcasts to promote Social Credit. The idea caught on like wildfire and he was invited to speak about it all over the province. Ultimately, candidates were selected to run in the 1935 provincial election, and his new political party won 56 of 63 seats in the Legislature.

In three short years Social Credit went from being an obscure economic theory to the guiding philosophy of a new political party dominating Alberta. University of Toronto professor John A. Irving explains that Aberhart himself was key to this success: "it is doubtful if the movement would have won political power in Alberta without his leadership" (Irving 1959, 337).

Needless to say, Aberhart's access to a large radio audience was an important factor in his ability to create and develop a political movement. It gave him a way to spread his message quickly and widely. Furthermore, he had considerable prestige as a popular religious leader. Those factors, though, were not sufficient for political success. As Irving writes, "the people of Alberta were also profoundly impressed by certain traits of leadership he possessed in addition to his religious influence. His presence and his voice, for example, contributed to inspire in his followers a fanatical and mysterious zeal: they felt that he spoke as one having authority" (Irving 1959, 258).

Aberhart's public speaking abilities were second-to-none. Accounts of his political meetings bring to mind the kinds of rallies held by Donald Trump in recent years. For example, during the 1935 provincial election campaign, the United Farmers of Alberta and Liberal Party candidates had trouble attracting audiences. Aberhart, by contrast, could draw large and enthusiastic crowds anywhere in the province.

As Irving recounts,

> Wherever he appeared, the roads leading to that place would be jammed with traffic all headed for the meeting place. The large audiences that always assembled would await his arrival with spontaneous expectancy. His appearance on the platform would be greeted with waves of thunderous applause. Even in small or remote villages like Sylvan Lake or Marwayne there was no relaxation of the heightening tempo of his campaign. The people who flocked to his meetings, invariably over-crowded, wanted a good show and they always got it. The great spellbinder never failed to lift his audiences to a state of hysterical enthusiasm (Irving 1959, 308).

In short, Aberhart was able to do what no other figure could do. He made a uniquely significant contribution to the political direction of Alberta. Irving writes, "previous to Aberhart's decision to take the Social Credit movement into politics, Alberta had never seen his like as a political leader. He was, indeed, a unique phenomenon, not only in the political experience of Alberta but in that of Canada at large" (Irving 1959, 258).

Quite simply, without the leadership of Bill Aberhart, it's very unlikely that Social Credit would have become a dominant force in Alberta politics. His particular leadership was a key factor.

To some degree, certain subsequent leaders have had a profound influence on Alberta politics as well. Peter Lougheed, for example, took a moribund provincial Progressive Conservative Party with no seats in the Legislature, and turned it into the governing party within six years. And in 1993, Ralph Klein delivered his "miracle on the prairies" when many knowledgeable observers believed that the days of the PC dynasty were finally over. Even the NDP election victory of 2015 is difficult to explain without acknowledging the leadership qualities of Rachel Notley. Of course, there is more to political success than leadership, but it can be the decisive factor in some cases, as it was for Social Credit.

When the right leader comes along advocating Alberta independence, the widespread but largely unaggregated support for renegotiating Alberta's place within Canada—or out of it—may come together into a powerful political force. Not long ago, Jason Kenney was able to "Unite Alberta" to rescue the province from the NDP, and he deserves credit for that. But now someone is needed to rescue the province from Ottawa. Like the early 1930s, the situation is getting desperate, and Alberta needs another special person to lead the fight for independence.

Whether or not such a leader emerges, Albertans must choose between the status quo and independence. Within Canada, Alberta's economy will be smothered by anti-oil policies and general hostility to resource development. Outside of Canada, Alberta's economy can flourish and supply much-needed energy to willing customers. This latter option will lead to prosperity for Albertans and their children. The choice is clear.

Vive l'Alberta libre!

REFERENCES

Albert, Richard. 2020. "Secession and Constitution in Alberta." *Moment of Truth: How to Think About Alberta's Future*, eds. Jack M. Mintz, Tom Flanagan, and Ted Morton, eds. Toronto: Sutherland House.

Angus Reid Institute. 2019. "Decades after Reform's rise, voters open to a new 'Western Canada Party.'" Vancouver. February 5.

Avramenko, Richard. 2013. "Of Homesteaders and Orangemen: An Archeology of Western Canadian Political Identity." *Hunting and Weaving: Empiricism and Political Philosophy*, eds. Thomas Heilke and John von Heyking. St. Augustine Press.

Banack, Clark. 2016. *God's Province: Evangelical Christianity, Political Thought, and Conservatism in Alberta*. McGill-Queen's University Press.

Banting, Keith, and Richard Simeon. 1983 "Preface." *And No One Cheered: Federalism, Democracy and the Constitution Act,* eds. Keith Banting and Richard Simeon. Toronto: Methuen Publications.

Barnes, Drew. 2020. Letter to Jason Kenney. June 16.

Bell, Edward. 2007. "Separatism and Quasi-Separatism in Alberta." *Prairie Forum*. Fall, pp. 335-356.

Bercuson, David and Barry Cooper 1994. *Derailed: The Betrayal of the National Dream*. Toronto: Key Porter Books.

Braid, Don. 2018. "Alberta's separatist sabres are rattling again." *Calgary Herald*. December 12: A6.

Braid, Don. 2020. "Declaration no joke." *National Post*. February 22: A10.

Byfield, Mike. "Preface." 1983. *The Deplorable Unrest in the Colonies: A Collection of Ted Byfield's Letters from the Publisher in Alberta Report*. Alberta Report.

Byfield, Ted. 1991a. "The Reform party: The timing was right." *Act of Faith*. Vancouver: British Columbia Report Books.

Byfield, Ted. 1991b. "Foreword." *The Great West Before 1900*. Volume 1 of Alberta in the 20th Century. Edmonton: United Western Communications Ltd.

Byfield, Ted. 1992. "Foreword." *The Birth of the Province 1900-1910*. Volume 2 of Alberta in the 20th Century. Edmonton: United Western Communications Ltd.

Byfield, Ted. 1998a. "Foreword." *Fury and Futility: The Onset of the Great Depression 1930-1935*. Volume 6 of Alberta in the 20th Century. Edmonton: United Western Communications Ltd.

Byfield, Ted. 1998b. "Foreword." *Aberhart and the Alberta Insurrection 1935-1940*. Volume 7 of Alberta in the 20th Century. Edmonton: United Western Communications Ltd.

Byfield, Ted. 1999. "Well, so far so good." *Alberta Report*. January 11.

Byfield, Ted. 2001a. "Of the West's four options, the first two take us down the path of Atlantic Canada." *The Report*. January 22.

Byfield, Ted. 2001b. "The West's paradox—the only way we can change Canada is by finding ways to leave it." *The Report*. February 5.

Cairns, Alan C. 1992. *Charter versus Federalism: The Dilemmas of Constitutional Reform*. Montreal & Kingston: McGill-Queen's University Press.

Campbell, Robert M., and Leslie A. Pal. 1989. *The Real Worlds of Canadian Politics: Cases in Process and Policy*. Peterborough: Broadview Press.

Cooper, Barry. 1984. "Western Political Consciousness." *Political Thought in Canada: Contemporary Perspectives*, ed. Stephen Brooks. Toronto: Irwin Publishing.

Cooper, Barry. 2009. *It's the Regime, Stupid! A Report from the Cowboy West on Why Stephen Harper Matters*. Key Porter Books.

Duffy, John. 2002. *Fights of Our Lives: Elections, Leadership, and the Making of Canada*. Toronto: HarperCollins Publishers Ltd.

Dumberry, Patrick. 2006. "Lessons learned from the Quebec Secession Reference before the Supreme Court of Canada." In *Secession: International Law Perspectives*, ed. Marcelo G. Kohen. Cambridge, UK: Cambridge University Press.

Elton, David and Roger Gibbins. 1979. "Western Alienation and Political Culture." *The Canadian Political Process*. Third Edition. eds. Richard Schultz, Orest M. Kruhlak and John C. Terry. Toronto: Holt, Rinehart and Winston of Canada, Limited.

Fair Deal Panel. 2020. *Report to Government*. Edmonton: Fair Deal Panel.

Fawcett, Max. 2020. "*The New Separatists.*" The Walrus. April.

Flanagan, Tom. 2020. "Alberta and the myth of Sisyphus." *Moment of Truth: How to Think About Alberta's Future*, eds. Jack M. Mintz, Tom Flanagan, and Ted Morton. Toronto: Sutherland House.

Flanagan, Tom, Jack Mintz, and Ted Morton. 2020. "A final word." *Moment of Truth: How to Think About Alberta's Future*, eds. Jack M. Mintz, Tom Flanagan, and Ted Morton. Toronto: Sutherland House.

Gibbins, Roger. 1982. *Regionalism: Territorial Politics in Canada and the United States*. Toronto: Butterworths (Canada) Limited.

Gibbins, Roger. 1983 "Constitutional Politics and the West." *And No One Cheered: Federalism, Democracy and the Constitution Act*, eds. Keith Banting and Richard Simeon. Toronto: Methuen Publications.

Gibbins, Roger. 1992. "Alberta and the National Community." In *Government and Politics in Alberta*, eds. Allan Tupper and Roger Gibbins. Edmonton: University of Alberta Press.

Gibbins, Roger and Loleen Berdahl. 2003. *Western Visions, Western Futures: Perspectives on the West in Canada*, Second Edition. Peterborough: Broadview Press.

Gilsdorf, Robert R. 1979. "Western Alienation, Political Alienation, and the Federal System: Subjective Perceptions." *Society and Politics in Alberta*, ed. Carlo Caldarola. Toronto: Methuen Publications.

Graney, Emma. 2018. "'Justice and equality' Fildebrandt says Alberta should consider separation if feds won't listen." *Edmonton Sun*. December 21: 6.

Graney, Emma. 2019. "Political left vs. right 'all hooey,' Independence Party leader says." *Edmonton Journal*. April 3: A2.

Harrison, Trevor. 1995. *Of Passionate Intensity: Right-Wing Populism and the Reform Party of Canada*. University of Toronto Press.

Huntington, Samuel P. 2005. *Who Are We? The Challenges to America's National Identity*. New York: Simon & Schuster Paperbacks.

Ibbitson, John. 2015. *Stephen Harper*. Toronto: Signal/McClelland & Stewart.

Ipsos Public Affairs. 2018. "Press Release: Western Alienation on the Rise? Not So Much." Vancouver. October 9.

Irving, John A. 1959. *The Social Credit Movement in Alberta*. Toronto: University of Toronto Press.

Johnson, William. 2006. *Stephen Harper and the Future of Canada*. Toronto: McClelland & Stewart.

Manning, Preston. 1992. *The New Canada*. Toronto: Macmillan Canada.

Mansell, Robert. 2020. "Alberta's fiscal contribution to confederation." *Moment of Truth: How to Think About Alberta's Future*, eds. Jack M. Mintz, Tom Flanagan, and Ted Morton. Toronto: Sutherland House.

McCormick, Peter, Ernest C. Manning, and Gordon Gibson. 1981. *Regional Representation: The Canadian Partnership*. Calgary: Canada West Foundation.

Mintz, Jack M. 2018. "Albexit: Bigger than Brexit." *Financial Post*. December 19: FP11.

Morin, Jacques-Yvan. 1999. "The Supreme Court Ruling: A Legitimate and Achievable Secession . . . in Theory." *The Quebec Decision: Perspectives on the Supreme Court Ruling on Secession*, ed. David Schneiderman. Toronto: James Lorimer & Company Ltd.

Morton, Ted. 1999. "Liberal Party Wins, Canada Loses." *The Quebec Decision: Perspectives on the Supreme Court Ruling on Secession*, ed. David Schneiderman. Toronto: James Lorimer & Company Ltd.

Morton, Ted. 2019. "Western separatism has moved past anger." *Calgary Herald*. October 26: A17.

Morton, Ted. 2020. "The status quo must go." *Moment of Truth: How to Think About Alberta's Future*, eds. Jack M. Mintz, Tom Flanagan, and Ted Morton. Toronto: Sutherland House.

Murphy, Rex. 2020a. "PM must choose: Paris or Calgary?" *National Post*. March 4: A8.

Murphy, Rex. 2020b. "Another slap in the face from Ottawa." *National Post*. December 17: A12.

Murphy, Rex. 2021. "Were I an Albertan, I'd be asking: What's the point?" *National Post*. January 23: A14.

Norrie, Kenneth H. 1979. "Some Comments on Prairie Economic Alienation." In *Society and Politics* in Alberta, ed. Carlo Caldarola. Toronto: Methuen Publications.

Norrie, Kenneth, and Michael Percy. 1981. "The Economics of a Separate West." *Western Separatism: The Myths, Realities & Dangers*, eds. Larry Pratt and Garth Stevenson. Hurtig Publishers.

Owram, Doug. 1981. "Reluctant Hinterland." *Western Separatism: The Myths, Realities & Dangers*, eds. Larry Pratt and Garth Stevenson. Edmonton: Hurtig Publishers.

Palmer, Howard and Tamara Palmer. 1990. *Alberta: A New History*. Edmonton: Hurtig Publishers.

Platt, Brian. 2021a. "Tory leadership rule change dulls Quebec's influence." *National Post*. March 20: A4.

Platt, Brian. 2021b. "Opening the door to federal intrusion." *National Post*. March 26: A1, A4.

Raymaker, Darryl. 2017. *Trudeau's Tango: Alberta Meets Pierre Elliott Trudeau, 1968-1972*. Edmonton: University of Alberta Press.

Reference re Secession of Quebec, [1998] 2 S.C.R. 217.

Reform Party of Canada. 1988. *Platform & Statement of Principles*. Edmonton: Reform Party of Canada.

Solomon, Lawrence. 2018. "Canada vs. the Republic of Alberta." *Financial Post*. December 7: FP9.

Staples, David. 2018. "From boom-time optimism to demands for separation." *Edmonton Journal*. December 12: A2.

Strom, Harry E. 1970. "The Feasibility of One Prairie Province." *One Prairie Province? Conference Proceedings and Selected Papers*, ed. David K. Elton. Lethbridge: Lethbridge Herald.

Thompson, Peter. 1969. *The Prairie Provinces: Alienation and Anger.* Toronto: McClelland and Stewart.

Wagner, Michael. 2009. *Alberta: Separatism Then and Now*. St. Catharines, ON: Freedom Press Canada Inc.

Wagner, Michael. 2012. *Leaving God Behind: The Charter of Rights and Canada's Official Rejection of Christianity*. Russell, ON: Christian Governance.

Wells, Paul. 2021. "True Blue Who?" *Maclean's*. March.

Wesley, Jared J. 2011. *Code Politics: Campaigns and Cultures on the Canadian Prairies*. Vancouver: UBC Press.

Wiseman, Nelson. 2007. *In Search of Canadian Political Culture.* Vancouver: UBC Press.

Woehrling, José. 1999. "The Quebec Secession Reference: Some Unexpected Consequences of Constitutional First Principles." *The Quebec Decision: Perspectives on the Supreme Court Ruling on Secession*, ed. David Schneiderman. Toronto: James Lorimer & Company Ltd.

Zeihan, Peter. 2014. *The Accidental Superpower: The Next Generation of American Preeminence and the Coming Global Disorder*. New York: Twelve/Hachette Book Group.

Acknowledgments

I would like to thank Derek Fildebrandt for inviting me to write for the Western Standard, where much of this material first appeared.

About the Author

Michael Wagner is an independent researcher and writer, and a columnist for the Western Standard. He has a BA (Honours) and MA in political science from the University of Calgary and PhD in political science from the University of Alberta. He has previously written the book, Alberta: Separatism Then and Now. He and his wife have eleven children.

CPSIA information can be obtained
at www.ICGtesting.com
Printed in the USA
BVHW082321050622
638842BV00002BA/10